GREAT BOOK OF MATH PUZZLES

Philip Heafford

D0104579

 Sterling Publishing Co., Inc.   New York

To all those who
love to solve a problem

Library of Congress Cataloging-in-Publication Data Available

10   9   8   7   6   5   4   3

Published in 1993 by Sterling Publishing Company, Inc.
387 Park Avenue South, New York, N.Y. 10016
Originally published in Great Britain
under the title *Mathematics for Fun*
© 1959, 1987 by Philip Heafford
Distributed in Canada by Sterling Publishing
% Canadian Manda Group, P.O. Box 920, Station U
Toronto, Ontario, Canada M8Z 5P9
Manufactured in the United States of America

Sterling ISBN 0-8069-8814-2

CONTENTS

1. Quickies

Do these numbers ring a bell? For instance, the number 365 would mean only one thing to me, and that is the number of days in a year. Ask someone to test you with this quiz. Six seconds for each question. How many can you get right in the time limit of two minutes for all the questions?

1. 1,760	11. .4771
2. 2,000	12. .4971
3. 4,840	13. 1.6
4. 640	14. 1.414
5. 1.732	15. 1,728
6. 2.54	16. 3-4-5
7. 3.1416 . . .	17. 6,080
8. 366	18. 62½
9. .3010	19. 90
10. 1492	20. 88

Answers on page 38.

2. The Printer's Nightmare

Before the days of the typewriter, the printer's lot was not always a happy one. Imagine how difficult it must have been for the unfortunate printer trying to set up the type for an arithmetic book when the hand-written manuscript was illegible. One printer overcame this difficulty by putting "stars" for the figures he could not decipher. See if you could have helped him by finding out what the figures really are.

1. Addition:

```
 ★22★          113
 1★★1          6★4
 ────          14★
 3489          ★26
 ────         ────
              ★410
              ────
```

2. Subtraction:

```
 4★★2          6★35
 ★35★          ★82★
 ────         ────
  121          4★7
 ────         ────
```

3. Multiplication:

```
  ★7          ★★★7
  ★★          ★★★
 ───         ────
 ★★★         ★★★★6
 ★★5         ★★203
 ───         ★37★★
 ★★91        ──────
 ────        ★★★★★★★
             ──────
```

4. Equations:

$5x - 5 = ★x - 3$ $x^2 - 4x = ★★$

$\therefore \; x = 2$ $\therefore \; x = 7$ or $★$

Answers on page 39.

3. Simple? Perhaps!

Can you solve these problems?

1. If five girls pack five boxes of flowers in five minutes, how many girls are required to pack fifty boxes in fifty minutes?

2. A boy has a long cardboard strip 1 inch wide and 48 inches long. It is marked at 1-inch intervals so that he can cut off a series of square inches. If the boy takes one second for each cut, how long will it take to cut the 48 square inches?

3. To move a safe, two cylindrical steel bars 7 inches in diameter are used as rollers. How far will the safe have moved forward when the rollers have made one revolution?

4. A town in India has a population of 20,000 people. 5 per cent of them are one-legged, and half the others go barefoot. How many sandals are worn in the town?

5. Without introducing + signs, arrange six "nines" in such a way that they add up to 100.

6. What is there peculiar about the left-hand side of $50\frac{1}{2} + 49\frac{38}{76} = 100$?

7. A fish had a tail as long as its head plus a quarter the length of its body. Its body was three-quarters of its total length. Its head was 4 inches long. What was the length of the fish?

Answers on pages 39–42.

4. Are You at Home in Rome?

For most of the answers to this quiz you will have to know the Roman figures. As they had no zero to give their numbers a "place value," it must have been very awkward when it came to multiplication!

1. What aid was used by the Romans to help with calculations?

2. The following is cut on a famous monument: MDCCLXXVI. What year does this represent?

3. Write 1789 in Roman figures.

4. What is the largest number you can write using these Roman numerals once each, I,C,X,V,L?

5. What is the smallest number you can write using the same Roman numerals once each, I,C,X,V,L?

6. Without changing to our Hindu-Arabic notation, find the value of CXVI + XIII + VI + CCLXV.

7. What Roman numbers of two integers between one and twenty become larger when the left-hand integer is omitted?

8. Was a "groma" used by the Roman merchant, surveyor, cook, or sailor?

Answers on pages 42–44.

5. Easy Teasers

1. During a vacation it rained on thirteen days, but when it rained in the morning the afternoon was fine, and every rainy afternoon was preceded by a fine morning. There were eleven fine mornings and twelve fine afternoons. How long was the vacation?

2. At what time between 7 and 8 o'clock will the two hands of a clock be in a straight line?

3. If $11^3 = 1,331$ and $12^3 = 1,728$, what is the cube root of the perfect cube 1,442,897?

4. A bottle of cider costs 25 cents. The cider cost 15 cents more than the bottle. How much should you receive on returning the bottle?

5. The lengths of the sides of a right-angled triangle measure an exact number of feet. If the hypotenuse is 1 foot longer than the base and the perpendicular is 9 feet long, how long are the sides?

6. A spruce tree when planted was 3 feet high and it grew by an equal number of feet each year. At the end of the seventh year, it was one-ninth taller than at the end of the sixth year. How tall was the tree at the end of the twelfth year?

7. Without doing the actual division state whether 13,972,536 is exactly divisible by 8.

8. A cement mixture costs $33 a ton. It is composed of Grade A cement at $36 a ton and Grade B cement at $24 a ton. How were these two cements mixed?

Answers on pages 44–46.

6. The Triangle Test

A triangle is a geometrical figure bounded by three straight lines and having three angles. Such a definition may be correct, but it gives one the idea that a triangle is a decidedly uninteresting figure. There are many different kinds of triangles and each one has its own interesting peculiarities. From the information given, can you state the names of these triangles?

1. I am readily suggested when you look at a trillium.

2. I appear when a man stands on level ground with his legs straight and his feet slightly apart.

3. I have a special name derived from a Greek word meaning "uneven."

4. I am formed by joining the feet of the perpendiculars from the vertices of a triangle to the opposite sides.

5. The sum of the squares on two of my sides equals the square constructed on my third side.

6. There are at least two of us. We find that our corresponding angles are equal and our sides are proportional.

7. The sides and the diagonals of a quadrilateral are used to construct me.

8. My sides are not straight lines and the sum of my angles is greater than 180°.

9. I have gained the title "pons asinorum" for a certain proposition in Euclid.

10. I am connected with the stars and the zenith.

Answers on pages 46–48.

7. Teasers

1. There are three books, each one inch thick. They stand side by side in order—Volumes I, II, and III. A bookworm starts outside the front cover of Volume I and eats its way through to the outside of the back cover of Volume III. If the worm travels in a straight line, how far does it travel?

2. A man built a cubical house with ordinary windows in all the upright walls. He found whenever he looked out of a window that he was looking south. Where did he build his house?

3. A merchant has two large barrels. The smaller barrel holds 336 liters but is only five-sixths full of wine. He empties this wine into the other barrel and finds that the wine fills only four-ninths of it. How much wine would the larger barrel hold when full?

4. What three curves are produced by making sections of a right circular cone in directions other than parallel to the base?

5. Two men play a card game and the stake is one penny a game. At the end one has won three games and the other has won three pennies. How many games did they play?

6. A number consists of three digits, 9, 5, and another. If these digits are reversed and then subtracted from the original number, an answer will be obtained consisting of the same digits arranged in a different order still. What is that other digit?

Answers on pages 48–49.

8. Some Old & Some New

1. Find a quantity such that the sum of it and one-seventh of it shall equal nineteen.

2. How many guests were present at a Chinese party if every two used a dish for rice between them, every three a dish for broth, every four a dish for meat, and there were 65 dishes altogether.

3. A retired colonel lived a quarter of his life as a boy, one-fifth as a young man, one-third as a man with responsibilities, and thirteen years on pension. How old was he when he died?

4. The fat men in a club outnumber the thin men by sixteen. Seven times the number of fat men exceeds nine times the number of thin men by thirty-two. Find the number of fat and thin men in the club.

5. An explorer grew a beard during his travels. At the end of his journeys, he found that double the length of his whiskers added to its square plus twenty exactly equalled the number of days he had been away. If he had measured the length of his beard in centimeters, and if he had been away 140 days, how long was his beard at the end of his travels?

6. A cathedral tower 200 feet high is 250 feet from a church tower 150 feet high. On the top of each tower is a pigeon. The two pigeons fly off at the same time and at the same speed directly to some grain on the level straight road between the towers. The pigeons reach the grain at the same instant. How far is the grain from the foot of the cathedral tower?

Answers on pages 49–51.

9. Spot the Mistakes

Merely because a statement appears in print it is not necessarily accurate! How often one hears the remark, "I'll show it to you in black and white," as if that is sufficient to decide whether something is true. A mathematician must always be accurate. Are the following statements true or false?

1. The pentagram of Pythagoras is formed by drawing all the diagonals of a regular pentagon.

2. Archimedes was the originator of the well-known puzzle of Achilles and the tortoise.

3. 1:05 p.m. is sometimes written as 1305 hours.

4. The curve in which a uniform cable hangs when suspended from two fixed points is a parabola.

5. A pantograph is a mechanical device for drawing figures similar to given figures.

6. A histogram is a hundred kilograms, and this standard unit is kept at the International Bureau of Weights and Measures at Sèvres, near Paris.

7. A cantilever beam is a beam supported at one end only and extending horizontally.

8. A parameter is an independent variable in terms of which the co-ordinates of a variable point may be expressed.

Answers on pages 51–53.

10. What's My Line?

For purposes of identification certain lines have been given special names, e.g. a tangent, an arc, and a radius. You have to name the line referred to in each of these questions. I . . .

1. join the vertex of a triangle to the mid-point of the opposite side.

2. was said to be the shortest distance between two points.

3. subtend a right angle at the circumference of a circle.

4. am the line so drawn in a circle that the angle between me and a certain tangent is equal to the angle in the alternate segment.

5. "touch" a hyperbola at an infinite distance.

6. cut a circle in two points.

7. join all the points of the same latitude on the earth.

8. am the locus of a point from which the tangents drawn to two given circles are equal.

9. am the essential straight line which, together with the special point or focus, enables points on an ellipse or parabola to be determined.

10. pass through the feet of the perpendiculars drawn to the three sides of a triangle from any point on the circumcircle of the triangle.

Answers on pages 53–55.

11. A Mathematical Mixture

This is a mixed bag of questions. Some are easy and some are hard. There is no connection between them whatsoever. Get busy as the proverbial bee and count how many you can answer correctly. Perfect marks will qualify you for the award of the Pythagorean star which you can draw for yourself. Do you know . . . ?

1. the number of barleycorns in an inch?

2. the instrument used by Sir Francis Drake to find the altitude of the sun and hence the time?

3. the instrument used in the sixteenth century to tell the time at night by observing the constellation Ursa Major?

4. the name of the mathematician who first proved
$$\triangle = \sqrt{s(s-a)(s-b)(s-c)}?$$

5. the name given to the figure like a five-pointed star often used in the Middle Ages to frighten away witches?

6. what "meter" is used to measure the area contained by a closed plane curve?

7. the name of the solid formed by cutting a pyramid or a cone by two parallel planes?

8. to what use Simpson's rule is put?

9. the common name for a regular hexahedron?

10. how long a clock will take to strike "twelve" if it takes five seconds to strike "six"?

Answers on pages 55–57.

12. Lighter Limericks

1. A dear old Grandpa named Lunn
   Is twice as old as his son.
      Twenty-five years ago
      Their age ratio
   Strange enough was three to one.

When does Grandpa celebrate his centenary?

2. Said a certain young lady called Gwen
   Of her tally of smitten young men,
      "One less and three more
      Divided by four
   Together give one more than ten."

How many boy friends had she?

3. There was a young fellow named Clive,
   His bees numbered ten to the power five.
      The daughters to each son
      Were as nineteen to one,
   A truly remarkable hive!

How many sons (drones) were in the hive?

4. A team's opening batter named Nero
   Squared his number of hits, the hero!
      After subtracting his score,
      He took off ten and two more,
   And the final result was a "zero."

How many hits did Nero make?

5. Some freshmen from Trinity Hall
   Played hockey with a wonderful ball;
      They found that two times its weight,
      Plus weight squared, minus eight,
   Gave "nothing" in ounces at all.

What was the weight of the ball?

Answers on pages 57–59.

13. A Math Medley

1. What is the name of the small metal frame with a glass or plastic front on which is a fine black line? It is used to facilitate the reading of a slide rule.

2. What is constructed in the same ratio as the following numbers? 24 : 27 : 30 : 32 : 36 : 40 : 45 : 48.

3. The minute hand of a clock is 7 inches long. What distance does the tip of the hand move in 22 minutes?

4. What curve has been called the "Helen of Geometers"?

5. How can you plant ten tulips in ten straight rows with three tulips in each row?

6. The diameter of a long-playing record is 12 inches. The unused center has a diameter of 4 inches and there is a smooth outer edge 1 inch wide around the recording. If there are 91 grooves to the inch, how far does the needle move during the actual playing of the recording?

7. Two men, Mr. Henry and Mr. Phillips, are appointed to similar positions. One elects to receive a beginning salary of $3,000 per year with increases of $600 each year, and the second, Mr. Phillips, chooses a beginning salary of $1,500 per half-year and an increase of $300 every six months. Which person is better paid?

Answers on pages 59–61.

14. "C" Gets the Worst of It

Below you will find some problems that were common in arithmetic textbooks fifty years ago. So often Mr. A, Mr. B, and Mr. C appeared, and the unfortunate Mr. C seemed to be the loser, or the person who got the worst of everything! If ever a single person deserves lasting credit from authors it is surely Mr. C. There are no rivals for that honor! Turn the clock back fifty years and solve the following:

1. A field is owned by three people; A has three fifths of it, and B has twice as much as C. What fraction of the field belongs to C?

2. In a mile race A beats B by 20 yards, and he beats C by 40 yards. By how much could B beat C in a mile race?

3. A and B can do a piece of work in ten days; A and C can do it in twelve days; B and C can do it in twenty days. How long will C take to do the work alone?

4. During a game of billiards A can give B 10 points in 50, and B can give C 10 points in 50. How many points in 50 can A give C to make an even game?

5. A, B, and C form a partnership. A furnishes $1,875, B furnishes $1,500, and C $1,250 capital. The partnership makes a profit of $1,850 in the first year. What should C take as his share of the profit?

6. Pipes A and B can fill a tank in two hours and three hours respectively. Pipe C can empty it in five hours. If all be turned on when the tank is empty, how long will it take to fill?

Answers on pages 61–63.

15. Letters for Numerals

Some simple sums were prepared using the numerals 0 to 9. Then all the numerals were changed to letters. You have to discover the code which was used for the change. You can do this if you look carefully for every possible clue. There is no need to guess. Work these clues methodically, trying each possibility one after the other. There is only one solution to each sum. The code has been changed for each sum. Don't peep at the answers until you have finished and checked your calculation, because the knowledge of one single change will make it too easy and spoil your fun.

1. Addition

```
    X X X X
    Y Y Y Y
    Z Z Z Z
  ───────────
    Y X X X Z
  ───────────
```

3. Division

```
            H I L
      I L )P H I L
           I L
          ────
            T I
            L S
          ────
          H I L
          H I L
          ────
            . . .
```

2. Multiplication

```
    P N X
      N X
  ─────────
    R N X
  N X S
  ─────────
  Z P N X
  ─────────
```

4. Division

```
              Y F Y
      A Y )N E L L Y
           N L Y
          ──────
            P P L
            P N H
          ──────
            N L Y
            N L Y
          ──────
              . . .
```

Answers on pages 63–65.

16. Some Short Stories

1. *When was it? Who was it?*

This is the story of a well-known man born years ago. He has influenced for many generations the thoughts and the minds of men and women in many different lands.

We can tell you that the first and last digits of the year during which he was born add up to the second digit, and that the third digit is one larger than the second digit, and that three times the fourth digit equals two times the third digit.

Can you calculate the year of his birth? Who is this gentleman?

2. *Who caught the bus?*

Juliette and her sister Lucile lived together in that beautiful town of Montreux by Lac Leman in the Swiss Alps. In the springtime one of their favorite walks was to go up to the lovely fields of narcissi growing on the mountain slopes nearby.

On one occasion they came to a long straight stretch of road, and at a certain point on it, they left the road and walked at right angles across a field to a large clump of narcissi. Juliette stopped to pick some of the flowers 40 meters away from the road, while Lucile also collected some flowers another meter farther on. Suddenly they looked up to see a bus going along the road to Montreux. When they had decided to ride home, the bus was 70 meters away from the point where they left the road to walk across the field.

They ran at half the speed the bus traveled to the point where they left the road and missed the bus! There is at least one point on that stretch of road where the bus could have been caught.

Can you calculate where they should have run and if both of the sisters could have caught the bus?

3. *How was this done?*

An Arab when he died left to his three sons seventeen camels, giving to the eldest one four ninths, to the second one third, and to the youngest one sixth of them. The three young men sat in front of their house contemplating how they could fulfill their father's wish without killing any of the animals. They did not find a solution to this problem. Suddenly a dervish came riding along on a camel. They asked him to sit down with them for a moment and told him of their troubles. The dervish pondered for a moment, smiled cunningly, and said, "I know how you can carry out your father's wish without having to kill even one of the animals."

Can you guess what suggestion the dervish made?

4. *Can a sheet of paper have one side only?*

The page on which this is printed has two sides and one edge all the way around. If you tear it out of the book you can easily trace the edge with a pencil. Nevertheless it would be a pity to spoil the book by doing this! If you want to go from one side of the paper to the other, you must go through the paper or over one of the edges.

Can you design a piece of paper that has only one side and also only one edge? If you can do this, then you can paint the whole surface with a brush (if the brush held enough paint) without removing it from the surface or going over an edge.

Answers on pages 65–67.

17. Brevity in Mathematics

The mathematician frequently uses abbreviations in his work. For the word "logarithms" he uses the shortened term "logs," and for "simple harmonic motion" he uses the initial letters of these words and writes "S.H.M." What abbreviation does he use for . . . ?

1. "which was to be proved or demonstrated"?

2. the cosine of the angle θ?

3. an expression which depends for its value on the value you give to x?

4. the integration of $16x^3$ with respect to x?

5. the smallest number which is exactly divisible by two or more numbers?

6. the hyperbolic sine of x?

7. the square root of -1?

8. the greatest number which will divide exactly into two or more numbers?

9. the derivative of y with respect to x?

10. the eccentricity of conics?

Answers on pages 67–69.

18. Was Charlie Coping?

Some rather surprising correct results are often found in Charlie's work, which frequently is good only in parts. Here are some examples from Charlie's homework. You have to correct these as quickly as possible. Are they right or wrong?

1. $12^2 = 144 \quad \therefore 21^2 = 441$

2. $13^2 = 169 \quad \therefore 31^2 = 961$

3. $\sqrt{5\frac{5}{24}} = 5\sqrt{\frac{5}{24}}$

4. $\sqrt[3]{2\frac{2}{7}} = 2\sqrt[3]{\frac{2}{7}}$

5. The lines joining the mid-points of the sides of a parallelogram form a parallelogram. Therefore the lines joining the mid-points of the sides of any convex quadrilateral also form a parallelogram.

6. $\text{Sin} \, (a + b) \cdot \sin \, (a - b) = (\sin a + \sin b)$
$$(\sin a - \sin b)$$
$$\therefore \sin \, (a + b) \cdot \sin \, (a - b) = \sin^2 a - \sin^2 b$$

7. Solve $\dfrac{x - 2}{y - 1} = \dfrac{3}{5}$ and $\dfrac{x - 1}{y} = \dfrac{2}{3}$

$$\therefore \frac{x - 1}{y} = \frac{x}{y} - 1 = \frac{2}{3}$$

$$\therefore \frac{x}{y} = \frac{2}{3} + 1 = \frac{5}{6}$$

$$\therefore x = 5, \text{ and } y = 6$$

8. How many triangles are there in this figure?
There are twelve lines.
Each triangle has three sides.

$$\therefore \frac{12}{3} = 4$$

$$\therefore 4 \times 4 = 16 \text{ triangles}$$

Answers on pages 69–70.

19. Can You Arrange These?

1. A boy is to be chosen president and a girl vice-president of the senior class of a school. In how many ways is this possible if the class has twelve boys and ten girls?

2. Six boys are to be photographed in a row. How many different arrangements can be made of the order in which they are to sit?

3. The same six boys are to sit around a table for lunch. How many different arrangements can be made of the order in which they are to sit?

4. If the first three letters of a telephone number indicate the name of the exchange, how many such arrangements of three letters is it possible to devise from the twenty-six letters of the alphabet?

5. How many different forecasts must be made of four football games in order to ensure that one forecast is correct?

6. In how many different ways can two dice, one red and one blue, come up when thrown?

7. One of the crews in the Harvard-Yale race has a problem for its captain. Three of the crew are stroke-side oarsmen only and two of them are bow-side oarsmen only. Ignoring weights and personal preferences, in how many ways can the captain arrange his eight men to form the crew? The cox is selected and does not change.

Answers on pages 71–73.

20. Puzzle These Out

1. A water lily doubles itself in size each day. From the time its first leaf appeared to the time when the surface of the pond was completely covered took forty days. How long did it take for the pond to be half covered?

2. A quart bottle had all its dimensions doubled. What is the volume of the new bottle?

3. From Philadelphia to Atlantic City is 60 miles. Two trains leave at 10:00 A.M., one train from Philadelphia at 40 miles an hour and the other from Atlantic City at 50 miles an hour. When they meet, are they nearer to Philadelphia or to Atlantic City?

4. Spot the wrong number in these series of numbers:
   (a) 1, 2, 4, 8, 15, . . .
   (b) 1, 7, 27, 64, 125, . . .
   (c) 10, 15, 21, 25, 30, . . .

5. What is the missing number in these series:
   (a) 81, 27, —, 3, 1, . . .
   (b) 1, 4, 9, —, 25, . . .
   (c) 2, 6, 12, —, 30, . . .

6. Which is the greatest and which the least of log $(2 + 4)$, $(\log 2 + \log 4)$, $\log (6 - 3)$, and $(\log 6 - \log 3)$?

7. Write down the Roman numerals from "one" to "six" as seen on a clock face.

Answers on pages 73–74.

21. Browsing in Books

It is always interesting to look at old books. You may have been fortunate enough to have seen some of the following in old arithmetic books. What could the author have meant by . . . ?

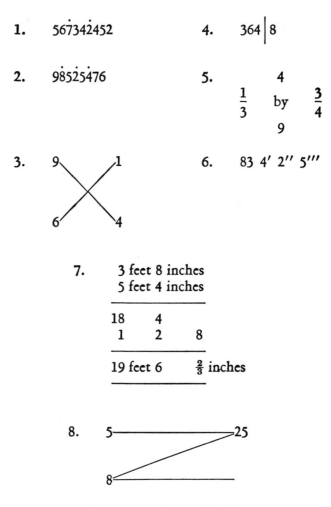

1.   5̇67342̇452

2.   98̇52̇547̇6

3.

4.   364 | 8

5.
$$\begin{array}{c} 4 \\ \frac{1}{3} \quad \text{by} \quad \frac{3}{4} \\ 9 \end{array}$$

6.   83 4' 2'' 5'''

7.

| 3 feet 8 inches | | |
5 feet 4 inches		
18	4	
1	2	8
19 feet 6	$\frac{2}{3}$ inches	

8.

Answers on pages 74–76.

22. Strange Figures Formed by Figures

```
                1
              1   1
            1   2   1
          1   3   3   1                    4   9   2
        1   4   6   4   1
      1   5   10  10  5   1                3   5   7
    1   —   —   —   —   —   1
  1   7   21  35  35  21  7   1            8   1   6
1   8   28  56  70  56  28  8   1
1   —   —   —   —   —   —   —   —   1
```

1. Write down the seventh line of figures in the arithmetical triangle.

2. What are the missing numbers in the last line of the arithmetical triangle?

3. Where in the arithmetical triangle do the coefficients of the terms of $(x + a)^2$ and $(x + a)^3$ appear?

4. Use the triangle to work out the coefficients of $(x + 2)^4$.

5. Who is the mathematician associated with this triangle?

6. Find the sum of the numbers in each column, each row, and each diagonal of the square printed above. What name is given to a square built in this way?

7. Complete a number square built in the same way as the one printed above, given:

16	2	12
6	—	—
8	—	—

8. Construct a number square of four rows and four columns such that the sum of each column, row, and diagonal is the same, and given that the top row is 1, 15, 14, and 4, and the left-hand column is 1, 12, 8, and 13.

Answers on pages 76–78.

23. Fun with Problems

1. The first five terms of the series 10, 20, 30, 40, 50 add up to 150. What five terms of another series, without fractions, add up to 153?

2. Find three vulgar fractions of the same value using all the digits 1 to 9 once only. Here is one solution of the problem:

$$\tfrac{3}{6} = \tfrac{7}{14} = \tfrac{29}{58}$$

3. A boy selling fruit has only three weights, but with them he can weigh any whole number of pounds from 1 pound to 13 pounds inclusive. What weights has he?

4. Can you, by adopting a mathematical process, such as $+$, $-$, $\times$, $\div$, $\sqrt{}$, etc., use all and only the digits 9, 9, 9 to make (a) 1, (b) 4, (c) 6?

5. From where on the surface of the earth can you travel 100 miles due south, then 100 miles due west, and finally 100 miles due north to arrive again at your starting point?

6. A train traveling at 60 miles an hour takes three seconds to enter a tunnel and a further thirty seconds to pass completely through it. What is the length of the (a) train, (b) tunnel?

Answers on pages 78–79.

24. Tackle These Twisters

Here you are faced with a succession of terms or quantities which, after the first term or quantity, are formed according to a common law. This sounds very complicated, but one grain of common sense plus two grains of confidence is all that is necessary to have some fun with the following series.

1. My reciprocals are in arithmetical progression, and I hope I am of some interest in the theory of sound. What is my name?

2. The ratios of successive terms of this series are connected with plant growth. The leaves of a head of lettuce and the layers of an onion grow like this. What is my name?

3. What is the sum of the first twenty terms of this series?

   $$1 + 3x + 5x^2 + 7x^3 + \cdots$$

4. What is the eighth term and also the sum of the first eight terms of this series?

   $$5 \cdot 7 \cdot 9 + 7 \cdot 9 \cdot 11 + 9 \cdot 11 \cdot 13 + 11 \cdot 13 \cdot 15 + \cdots$$

5. Is the logarithmic series,

   $$\log_e (1 + x) = x - \frac{x^2}{2} + \frac{x^3}{3} - \frac{x^4}{4} + \cdots$$

   useful for working out logarithms to the base e?

6. What is the name of this series?

   $$x - \frac{x^3}{3!} + \frac{x^5}{5!} - \frac{x^7}{7!} + \cdots$$

7. What is the name of this series?

   $$1 + x + \frac{x^2}{2!} + \frac{x^3}{3!} + \cdots + \cdots$$

Answers on pages 79–81.

25. Some Statistical Studies

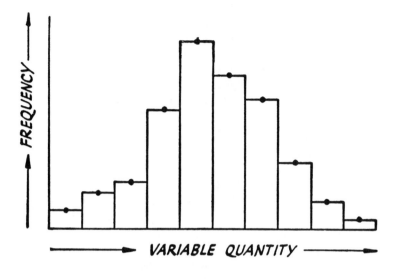

What is the name of . . .

1. this special column graph?

2. the shape formed by joining the mid-points of the tops of the columns?

3. the frequency curve shaped like a cocked hat?

4. the arithmetical average of the values of a variable quantity?

5. the most frequently observed value of a variable quantity?

6. that which most satisfactorily indicates the spread of the observed values of a variable quantity?

7. the sample chosen such that every sample has an equal chance of being picked?

Answers on pages 81–83.

26. A Few Fast Ones

1. How far can you go into a forest?
2. A man drives along a main highway on which a regular service of buses is in operation. He notices that every three minutes he meets a bus and that every six minutes a bus overtakes him. How often does a bus leave the terminal station at one end of the route?
3. There are twelve dollars in a dozen. How many dimes are there in a dozen?
4. An airplane flies around the equator at a constant height of 200 feet. If the radius of the earth is 4,000 miles how much farther than the circumference of the earth will the airplane have to travel?
5. In a small town of 50,000 inhabitants, it has been counted that 42 per cent of the males and 28 per cent of the females married people from their own town. Assuming these numbers have remained fairly constant over the years, how many males are there in the town?
6. You are standing at the center of a circle of radius 9 feet. You begin to hop in a straight line to the circumference. Your first hop is $4\frac{1}{2}$ feet, your second $2\frac{1}{4}$ feet, and you continue to hop each time half the length of your previous hop. How many hops will you make before you get out of the circle?
7. Three students have two boxes of candy which they want to share equally among themselves. Neither the number of pieces in the first box nor the number in the second is divisible by three. Yet one of the students noticed that there were seven more pieces in the second box than in the first and then he said, "We can share this candy equally between us." Was he correct?

Answers on pages 83–85.

27. Calculus Cocktails

There are some problems which anyone with an elementary knowledge of calculus can solve with the utmost ease. After a short time a beginner can tackle interesting and practical problems. The feeling of accomplishment, and even fun, which the subject brings when rightly used is also increased by the beauty of its methods. Below are four problems which can be solved by the aid of this admirable instrument.

1. A hiker on the moors is 2 miles from the nearest point, *P*, on a straight road. 8 miles from *P* along the road is an inn. The hiker can walk at 3 miles per hour over the grassy moors and at 5 miles per hour along the good road. At what distance from *P* must he aim to strike the road in order to get to the inn as quickly as possible?

2. Dan Dare the space-ship pilot wears a space hat in the shape of a paraboloid of revolution. The diameter of the circular base is 8 inches and the height of the hat is 12 inches. What volume of heavy water will it hold?

3. Equal squares are cut out at each of the corners of a rectangular sheet of tinfoil whose dimensions are 32 inches by 20 inches. Find the maximum volume of a wooden box which can be lined by suitably bending the tinfoil to cover the base and the sides of the box.

4. A pleasure steamer 150 feet long has changed its direction through 30 degrees while moving through a distance equal to twice its own length. What is the radius of the circle in which it moved?

Answers on pages 85–88.

28. Track the Term

There are a large number of mathematical terms that are included in expressions in common use. How frequently we hear "equal rights," "shooting a line," "hot rod," "100-percent effort," "integral part," "vicious circle." You will be able to find many more if you listen carefully. In the following, find the mathematical term that is a part, or the whole, of an everyday expression suggested by:

1. The area over which anything exerts influence.

2. Having equal scores when playing golf.

3. The hour at which an operation is timed to begin.

4. The Great —— between Atlantic and Pacific.

5. A phrase implying excess and having no relation in size, amount, etc.

6. The modern measuring unit of intelligence.

7. A famous military building.

8. One who sets forth in words, expounds, or interprets.

9. The rejection of a person proposed for some office.

10. A judge recapitulates the evidence at the end of a case.

Answers on pages 88–89.

29. Arches

The application of geometry to architectural drawings is obvious, and a mathematician can be an interesting companion on a sight-seeing tour. One thrilled a group of students when he showed them how a particular arch in an old church could be drawn readily with the aid of a pair of compasses and a ruler. Can you spot the arch that is suggested by the following statements?

1. It sounds like an exclamation, but is an arch of two double curves that rise to a point.

2. It is common in Early English churches, and is also the name of a surgical instrument.

3. Very good food is suggested! The Mohammedan race inhabiting Northwest Africa never used this arch.

4. This arch is not connected with heraldry, but is used to support a flight of solid steps.

5. Obviously very much connected with a certain kind of triangle.

6. The commonest brick arch in house construction.

7. A rounded arch of more than a semicircle.

8. Most likely to be found in spacious buildings constructed in England between 1485 and 1546.

9. I am semicircular in shape and often have a chevron ornamentation.

Answers on pages 90–92.

30. Circles, Circles & More Circles

Given the following clues, can you name the circle which is implied?

1. It seems to be "a manager," but the two tangents from any point on it to an ellipse are at right angles.

2. It seems as if this circle could be helpful to an ellipse.

3. Is a circle very much tied up with the feet of the altitudes and the mid-points of the sides of a triangle. What size shoe did Clementine wear?

4. Two circles which cut "right" across each other.

5. The circle which touches all the sides of a polygon.

6. King Alfred did not really name this circle!

7. The circle which seems to be suffering from "spring fever."

8. A triangle is greedy enough to have more than one of these circles.

9. A circle which passes through the vertices of a triangle.

Answers on pages 92–94.

ANSWERS

1. Quickies

1. Yards in 1 mile.

2. Pounds in 1 ton.

3. Square yards in 1 acre.

4. Acres in 1 square mile.

5. The square root of 3.

6. Centimeters in an inch.

7. π—the ratio of the circumference of a circle to its diameter.

8. Days in a leap year.

9. The logarithm of 2 to the base 10.

10. The year in which Christopher Columbus found land (in the Bahamas) by sailing west from Spain.

11. The logarithm of 3 to the base 10.

12. The logarithm of π to the base 10.

13. 1.6 kilometer = 1 mile, and 0.6214 mile = 1 kilometer.

14. The square root of 2.

15. Cubic inches in 1 cubic foot.

16. Ratio of the sides of a right-angled triangle.

17. Feet in a nautical mile.

18. $62\frac{1}{2}$ pounds is the weight of 1 cubic foot of water.

19. Degrees in 1 right angle.

20. 88 feet per second is the same as 60 miles per hour.

2. The Printer's Nightmare

1.   2228
     1261
     ─────
     3489
     ─────

          113
          624
          147
          526
        ─────
       1410
       ─────

2.   4472
     4351
     ─────
      121
     ─────

     6235
     5828
     ─────
      407
     ─────

3.   47
      53
     ────
     141
     235
     ────
   2491
     ────

     5467
      898
     ────
   43736
   49203
   43736
   ────────
 4909366
   ────────

4. $5x - 5 = 4x - 3$ $x^2 - 4x = 21$
     $\therefore \; x = 2$ $\therefore \; x = 7 \text{ or } -3$

3. Simple? Perhaps!

1. *FIVE GIRLS*
Five girls pack five boxes in five minutes,
Five girls pack one box in one minute (working on the same box!),
Five girls pack fifty boxes in fifty minutes.

2. 47 SECONDS

The time taken will be 47 seconds, because the 47th cut produces the last two squares.

3. 44 INCHES

Steel bars are often used as rollers in this way. The safe moves forward twice the length of the circumference of one of the steel bars. This distance is therefore $\dfrac{2 \cdot 22 \cdot 7}{7}$ inches, which is 44 inches. With three or any number of rollers under the safe it will still move forward 44 inches. The best way to see this is to consider this problem in two parts:

(a) the motion forward caused by one revolution of the rollers if they were rolling off the ground,

(b) the motion forward of the centers of the rollers because they themselves roll forward on the ground.

In both cases the motion amounts to 22 inches, so that the total movement of the safe mounted on the rolling rollers is 44 inches.

4. 20,000

Did you get this right? It really does not matter what percentage of the population is one-legged! All the one-legged people will require only one shoe in any case. Of the remainder, half will wear no shoes and the other half will carry two shoes on their two feet. This works out at one shoe per person for the "others." We shall therefore need for the whole population on the average one shoe per person.

5. $99\dfrac{99}{99}$

This is one of the old trick problems. If recognized signs

were introduced, you could arrange six "nines" to give 100 as follows:

$$[(9 \times 9) + 9] + 9\frac{9}{9}$$

You could also arrange four "nines" to give 100 as follows:

$$99\frac{9}{9}$$

6. *ALL THE NUMBERS 0 TO 9 APPEAR*

This is interesting, but it is by no means the only example of composing 100 from all the numbers 0 to 9 taken once only. Examine these solutions:

(a) $0 + 1 + 2 + 3 + 4 + 5 + 6 + 7 + (8 \times 9)$

(b) $78\frac{3}{6} + 21\frac{45}{90}$

(c) $89 + 6\frac{1}{2} + 4\frac{35}{70}$

(d) $90 + 8\frac{3}{6} + 1\frac{27}{54}$

(e) $1 + 2\frac{35}{70} + 96\frac{4}{8}$

(f) $97\frac{30}{45} + 2\frac{6}{18}$

(g) $97\frac{43}{86} + 2\frac{5}{10}$

Can you design still more solutions?

7. *128 INCHES*

Let H represent the head, B the body, T the tail, and L the total length of the fish.

Looking at the problem we are given the following three facts:

$$T = H + \tfrac{1}{4}B$$
$$B = \tfrac{3}{4}L$$
$$H = 4 \text{ inches}$$

It is also true that $L = H + B + T$

In this equation keep L and substitute for everything else.

$$\therefore\ L = 4\ \text{inches} + \tfrac{3}{4}L + (H + \tfrac{1}{4}B)$$
$$\therefore\ L = 4\ \text{inches} + \tfrac{3}{4}L + 4\ \text{inches} + \tfrac{3}{16}L$$
$$\therefore\ L = 8\ \text{inches} + \tfrac{15}{16}L$$
$$\therefore\ \tfrac{1}{16}L = 8\ \text{inches}$$
$$\therefore\ L = 8 \times 16\ \text{inches}$$
$$\therefore\ L = 128\ \text{inches}$$

Thus we see that the fish was 128 inches long.

4. Are You at Home in Rome?

1. THE ABACUS

The merchants and traders of ancient days in Egypt and Mesopotamia used to set out pebbles in grooves of sand to calculate and add up accounts. There would be a "units" groove, a groove for "tens," and one for "hundreds." Such was a simple abacus, and the word is derived from a Greek word meaning "tablet." In Roman times, a calculating frame was made in which pebbles slid on wires and this was also called an abacus. The size of the abacus determined the size of the numbers which could be dealt with. The Roman numerals made simple addition, subtraction, and multiplication very complicated. Calculations were done by slaves using an abacus. It is interesting to note that the Roman word for "pebble" was "calculus" and here we have the derivation of our word "calculate."

2. 1776

Letters were used by the Romans to represent various numbers, and they seem to follow the pattern set by the Greeks.

1, 5, 10, 50, 100, 500, 1000
I, V, X, L, C, D, M

The Roman numerals on the monument therefore read as:

M = 1000, D = 500, C = 100, C = 100, L = 50, X = 10, X = 10, V = 5, I = 1

These added together make 1776, and every American knows this date!

3. *MDCCLXXXIX*

M = 1000, D = 500, C = 100, C = 100, L = 50, X = 10, X = 10, X = 10, and IX = 9. Add these all together and the result is 1789.

4. *CLXVI*
This number is 166.

5. *CXLIV*
This number is 144. XL is ten before fifty, which is forty. Similarly, IV is one before five, which is four.

6. *CD*

C	X	VI
	X	III
		VI
CC	LX	V
CD		

The answer of the addition is four C's, which is four hundred. It was the custom not to write four similar numerals consecutively. Hence, instead of writing four "hundreds" (CCCC), the Romans wrote one hundred less than five hundred (CD). Placing the C before the D meant C less than D, and placing it after the D, as in DC, meant C more than D. So that CD is four hundred and DC is six hundred.

7. 4 *and* 9
The Roman numeral for four is IV. Therefore, when the left-hand integer is removed there remains the integer V. V is the Roman numeral for five. Hence the four changes to five. Similarly, the Roman numeral for nine is IX, and when the left-hand integer I is removed there remains the Roman numeral X, which is ten.

8. SURVEYOR

The "groma" was an important surveying instrument used by the Roman surveyors or agrimensores. As far as mathematics was concerned, the Romans were practical and no more. To them mathematics was a tool that helped them to construct and to measure. The agrimensor was a land- or field-measurer, and in this work he used the groma. It was frequently carved on the tombstones of Roman surveyors.

5. Easy Teasers

1. 18 DAYS

There are three possible types of day:

    (a) Rain in the morning and fine in the afternoon
    (b) Fine in the morning and rain in the afternoon
    (c) Fine in the morning and fine in the afternoon

Let the number of such days in each category be a, b, and c.
$\therefore$ number of days on which rain falls $= a + b = 13$
$\therefore$ number of days having fine mornings $= b + c = 11$
$\therefore$ number of days having fine afternoons $= a + c = 12$

From these equations, we derive that $a = 7$, $b = 6$, and $c = 5$.
$\therefore$ number of days on vacation is $7 + 6 + 5 = 18$.

2. $5\frac{5}{11}$ MINUTES PAST 7

At 7 o'clock the minute hand is 35 divisions behind the hour hand.

To be opposite one another the minute hand must gain 5 divisions on the hour hand.

But the minute hand gains 55 divisions in 60 true minutes.
$\therefore$ the minute hand gains 5 divisions in $5\frac{5}{11}$ true minutes.

All problems concerning the positions of the hands on clock faces will be solved readily if you draw a sketch and remember that the accurate position is "something" and "something"-elevenths.

3. 113

1,442,897 is a seven-figure number and thus the cube root must lie between 110 and 120. As the last figure is a 7, the cube root must end in 3.

4. FIVE CENTS

Let your algebra help you!
$$C + B = 25$$
$$C = 15 + B$$
$$\therefore B = 5.$$

5. 9, 40, *and* 41 FEET

The procedure is as follows: square the length of the perpendicular, subtract 1, divide by 2. The result is the length of the base. Add 1 and then that is the length of the hypotenuse. This applies when the perpendicular is any odd number and these combinations of numbers are sometimes called Pythagorean series. Other combinations are 3-4-5, 5-12-13, 7-24-25, 11-60-61, 13-84-85, and so on indefinitely. The method is derived from the theorem of Pythagoras concerning a right-angled triangle.

$$H^2 = B^2 + P^2$$
$$\therefore (B + 1)^2 = B^2 + P^2$$
$$\therefore 2B + 1 = P^2$$
$$\therefore B = \frac{P^2 - 1}{2}$$

6. 15 FEET

Let the tree grow x feet each year.
At the end of the sixth year, the height of the tree
$$= (3 + 6x) \text{ feet}$$
$$\text{The growth } x = \tfrac{1}{9}(3 + 6x)$$
$$\therefore x = \tfrac{1}{3} + \tfrac{2}{3}x$$
$$\therefore x = 1$$
At the end of the twelfth year, the height
$$\text{of the tree} = (3 + 12x) \text{ feet}$$
$$= 15 \text{ feet.}$$

45

7. YES

Do you know the tests of divisibility? Numbers will divide exactly

by 2 if they end with an even digit
    " 3 if the sum of the digits is divisible by 3
    " 4 if the last two digits are divisible by 4
    " 5 if the last digit is 0 or 5
    " 6 if divisible by both 2 and 3
    " 8 if the last three digits are divisible by 8

What about the tests of divisibility for 7, 9, 11, and 12?

8. GRADE A: GRADE B = 3 : 1

Let A parts of Grade A be mixed with B parts of Grade B cement, then the equation is:

$$36A + 24B = 33\,(A + B)$$
$$\therefore\ 3A = 9B$$
$$\therefore\ \frac{A}{B} = \frac{3}{1}$$

6. The Triangle Test

1. EQUILATERAL

As the name suggests, all the sides are equal. Equilateral triangles have not only equal sides but have equal angles too and can thus be called equiangular triangles. The trillium has three axes of symmetry suggesting an equilateral triangle. Many plants have geometrical shapes in their roots, stems, leaves, and flowers. What shape is found in the cross-section of the stem of the sedge family?

2. ISOSCELES

The word means "equal legs." Any triangle which has two of its three sides equal is called an isosceles triangle. If we look around us we can often find geometrical figures in nature. In the construction of houses, ships, and aircraft, the isosceles triangle is often encountered.

46

3. SCALENE
This is a triangle which is "uneven" because it has all its sides unequal. The word "scalene" has nothing to do with drawing to scale, but is derived from the Greek word "*skalenos*," which means "uneven" or "unequal."

4. PEDAL
This triangle is sometimes called the orthocentric triangle. If *AD*, *BE*, and *CF* are the perpendiculars dropped from the vertices of the triangle *ABC* to the opposite sides, then the triangle *DEF* is the pedal triangle. The three perpendiculars pass through a common point called the orthocenter.

5. RIGHT-ANGLED
The unique property of the right-angled triangle *ABC* is that if angle *A* is the right angle then $a^2 = b^2 + c^2$. The geometrical proof of this property is associated with the Greek mathematician Pythagoras, who lived in the sixth century B.C. Triangles whose sides are in the ratios 3-4-5 or 5-12-13 are right-angled.

6. SIMILAR
Two triangles are said to be similar if they have their angles equal to one another and have their sides, taken in order, about the corresponding equal angles proportional. The areas of similar triangles are proportional to the squares of their corresponding sides.

7. HARMONIC
ABCD is the quadrilateral and *OXY* is the harmonic triangle. It is formed by joining the intersection points of the sides and the intersection point of the diagonals.

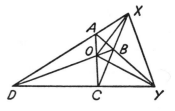

8. SPHERICAL
A spherical triangle consists of a portion of a sphere bounded by three arcs of great circles. Obviously the sides do not consist of straight lines. The sum of the three angles of such a

triangle lies between 180° and 540°. Much of the early work with spherical triangles was done by Menelaus about A.D. 100.

9. *ISOSCELES*
The particular proposition proved that the angles at the base of an isosceles triangle are equal. The title "pons asinorum" means the "bridge of asses." It is said that in the Middle Ages the "donkey" could not pass over this bridge to continue his study of Euclidean geometry, but the name may be due to the fact that the figure in Euclid resembles a simple truss bridge.

10. *ASTRONOMICAL*
This is a spherical triangle on a celestial sphere which has for its vertices the nearest celestial pole, the zenith, and the star under consideration.

7. Teasers

1. *ONE INCH*
Surely the bookworm has only to go from A to B as in the figure! This distance is the thickness of Volume II—one inch.

2. *THE NORTH POLE*
One cannot imagine that there is a cubical igloo at the North Pole! But if there were and if it had windows they would all have a southern outlook.

3. 630 *LITERS*
Let x be the volume of the second barrel. Your equation will be:

$$\frac{5}{6} \times 336 = \frac{4}{9} \times x$$

$$\therefore \ x = \frac{5 \times 336 \times 9}{6 \times 1 \times 4}$$

4. ELLIPSE, PARABOLA, HYPERBOLA

These three curves are often referred to as "conic sections." The sections are shown in the figure—the hyperbola is parallel to the axis, the parabola is parallel to the slant height, and the ellipse is oblique. The base is, of course, a circle.

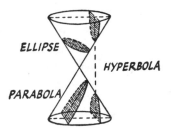

5. NINE

A wins three games and thus gains three pennies. B has to win back these three pennies which takes another three games, and finally B wins three more games to win the total sum of three pennies.

6. 4

If x = the missing digit, then the solution is found from this equation:

$$900 + 50 + x - (100x + 50 + 9) = 100x + 90 + 5$$

Thus the number is 954, and $954 - 459 = 495$.

8. Some Old & Some New

1. 16⅝

This problem is to be found in the ancient Rhind papyrus or Ahmes papyrus written more than a thousand years before Christ. The original wording appears strange: "heap, its seventh, its whole, it makes nineteen."

The solution is found thus:

$$x + \frac{x}{7} = 19$$

$$\therefore\ 8x = 133$$
$$\therefore\ x = 16\tfrac{5}{8}$$

2. 60

This problem is traditionally attributed to Sun Tsu, who lived in the first century A.D. His method of solving the problem did not involve the usual unknown quantity "x." He did not give us the solution but only the answer—perhaps he guessed. The modern solution is:

Let $x =$ the number of guests.

Equating the number of dishes from the information given,

$$\frac{x}{2} + \frac{x}{3} + \frac{x}{4} = 65$$

$$\therefore\ 6x + 4x + 3x = 65 \times 12$$
$$\therefore\ 13x = 65 \times 12$$
$$\therefore\ x = 60$$

3. 60 YEARS

This is an example of the type of problem which was popular in the fourth century. It is easily solved by letting his age be represented by x years.

$$\text{Then } \frac{x}{4} + \frac{x}{5} + \frac{x}{3} = x - 13$$

$$\therefore\ 15x + 12x + 20x = 60x - (60 \times 13)$$
$$\therefore\ x = 60$$

4. 56 FAT MEN and 40 THIN MEN

To solve this problem, all we need to do is to put the story down in mathematical symbols thus:

$$F - 16 = T \qquad \ldots\ldots 1$$
$$7F - 32 = 9T \qquad \ldots\ldots 2$$

Multiply line *1* by 9:

$$9F - 144 = 9T \qquad \ldots\ldots 3$$

Take line 2 away from line 3:

$$\therefore\ 2F - 112 = 0$$
$$\text{Hence}\ \ F = 56$$
$$\text{and}\ \ T = 40$$

5. 10 CENTIMETERS—*not too long!*

Translate this problem into mathematical symbols and then there is an easy quadratic equation to be solved.
Let the length of beard be L centimeters.

$$2L + L^2 + 20 = 140$$
$$L^2 + 2L - 120 = 0$$
$$(L + 12)(L - 10) = 0$$
$$\text{Hence}\ \ L = 10 \text{ centimeters}$$

6. 90 FEET

Applying the theorem of Pythagoras to both of the right-angled triangles:

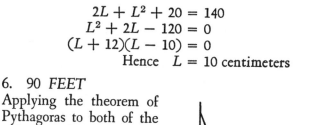

$$y^2 = 200^2 + x^2$$
$$y^2 = 150^2 + (250 - x)^2$$
$$\therefore\ 40,000 + x^2 =$$
$$22,500 + 62,500$$
$$- 500x + x^2$$
$$\therefore\ 500x = 45,000$$
$$\therefore\ x = 90$$

9. Spot the Mistakes

1. TRUE

The pentagram of Pythagoras is the five-pointed star formed by drawing all the diagonals of a regular pentagon and deleting the sides. Pentagrams, heptagrams, and nonograms were considered at a very early date to have magical and mystical properties. The pentagram in particular was used as a symbol of health and happiness. The Pythagoreans (disciples of Pythagoras) used the pentagram as their badge of recognition.

2. FALSE

Zeno was the originator of the paradox of Achilles and the tortoise. Zeno of Elea lived in the fifth century B.C., and he has been associated with many paradoxes of time, space, and motion. Zeno argued that no matter how fast Achilles ran he could never catch the tortoise, for the latter would move a short distance on as Achilles covered the distance between him and where the tortoise was!

3. TRUE

The sensible means of avoiding any confusion between A.M. and P.M. is to use the twenty-four-hour clock. The railway timetables on the continent of Europe leave no possible doubt about the time of the day or night when a train is due to leave a station. Midnight is expressed as 0000 hours and every time during the day is expressed in four digits. For instance, 9:30 A.M. = 0930 hours, and 12 noon = 1200 hours, and 4:15 P.M. = 1615 hours.

4. FALSE

The curve assumed by a chain, rope, or cable when hanging freely between two supports is very much like a parabola, but is really quite different. The curve is called a catenary, which is derived from the Latin word "catena," a chain. Galileo thought this curve was a parabola, and it was not until late in the seventeenth century that the Bernoullis and Leibnitz discovered the peculiar properties of the catenary.

5. TRUE

The pantograph can be used to copy any figure composed of any combination of straight lines and curved lines. It can be adjusted to cause the copy to be of the same size or to be enlarged or reduced. The instrument consists essentially of a freely-jointed parallelogram of hinged rods. The lengths of the sides of the parallelogram are varied to produce the different sizes of the copy. The original and the copy are in two dimensions and lie in the same plane.

6. FALSE

A histogram is in no way connected with the unit of weight, the gram. It is true that the metric standards are kept at the International Bureau of Weights and Measures at Sèvres near Paris. The histogram is connected with the method of graphical representation of data, and is described elsewhere in this book.

7. TRUE

In architecture the cantilever is a projecting bracket which is used to support a balcony. There are very many examples of its use in buildings of several generations. It is also of great use in the building of bridges. Two cantilevers stretch out from piers on opposite sides and these are joined together by a girder to complete the span. The Quebec Bridge over the St. Lawrence River in Canada has the longest cantilever span in the world—1,800 feet.

8. TRUE

This is the way in which the term "parameter" is used in mathematics when dealing with the equations of curves and surfaces. It came into use about a hundred years ago. The use of parametric equations frequently simplifies calculations in algebraic geometry and calculus. Parameter means a "side measure." For instance, the co-ordinates of a point on a parabola expressed in terms of one parameter "t" can be written as at^2, $2at$.

10. What's My Line?

1. MEDIAN

This is the definition which is usually given of a median. The three medians of a triangle are concurrent, and the point at which they intersect is one third of the way along each median measured toward the vertex from the mid-point of the opposite side.

2. STRAIGHT LINE

This was the old definition of a straight line. It is doubtful whether a navigator would agree with this entirely, but as far as mathematics is concerned this is the meaning usually attached to it in simple geometry. A better definition would be "a straight line is one which keeps the same direction throughout its length."

3. DIAMETER

The diameter of a circle is a straight line drawn through the center and terminated at both ends by the circumference. Any diameter cuts a circle into two equal parts, each being called a semicircle. The angle in a semicircle is a right angle.

4. CHORD

An important theorem in geometry states that if a tangent be drawn to a circle and at the point of contact a chord be drawn, then the angles which the chord makes with this tangent are equal to the angles in the alternate segments of the circle.

5. ASYMPTOTE

This peculiar word is derived from the Greek language and first appeared in mathematics in 1656. It was used for the name of the line to which a curve continually approaches but does not meet within a finite distance. Frequently an asymptote is called a tangent at infinity.

6. SECANT

If a straight line cuts any curve at two distinct points, it is called a secant. The beginner in geometry must always differentiate between a secant and a tangent, for the latter, no matter how far it is produced either way, has only one point in common with a curve.

7. PARALLEL OF LATITUDE

This is a small circle drawn through places of the same latitude. It is parallel to the equator and at right angles to the earth's axis or the line joining the North and South Poles. Latitudes are expressed in degrees and minutes on either side north or south of the equator.

8. RADICAL AXIS
This is the locus or path of a point which moves so that the tangents drawn from it to two fixed circles are equal. Actually it is a straight line perpendicular to the line joining the centers of the two circles.

9. DIRECTRIX
The term came into use in 1702. The distance from any point on a conic (ellipse or parabola) to the directrix bears a constant ratio to the distance of the same point from the focus of the conic. For determining the standard equation for a conic the directrix–focus property is generally used.

10. SIMSON or PEDAL LINE
Robert Simson, professor of mathematics at Glasgow University in the eighteenth century, has been honored by having this particular line of a triangle named after him. He made many contributions to mathematics, and most of the English editions of Euclid are based on his work.

11. A Mathematical Mixture

1. THREE
Early linear measurements were defined in terms of body sizes which, of course, vary from man to man! The earliest English law defining length was made during the reign of Edward II in 1324. It read, "Three barley corns, round and dry, placed end to end, make an inch." Probably this was more of a standard than the width of a man's thumb.

2. ASTROLABE
The name is derived from two Greek words meaning "star

taking," but the instrument can be used to take the altitude of the sun or moon. By the fifteenth century, quite complicated astrolabes were being used by astronomers, but about 1480 a simpler instrument was made for mariners. The mariner had to know the sun's declination from tables and he could then calculate his latitude from his own observation of the altitude of the midday sun using the astrolabe. This instrument did not give accurate results and in the eighteenth century it was superseded by Hadley's sextant. The maximum angle which could be measured by Hadley's sextant was 90°, hence it was sometimes called a quadrant.

3. NOCTURNAL
A nocturnal is an instrument which was used for finding the time by night by observing the relative positions of the North Star and the pointers of the Big Dipper. In the British Museum can be seen a nocturnal made by Humfray Cole in 1560. This instrument was not difficult to use, and when the movable arm was adjusted so that the two pointers of the Big Dipper appeared to lie on it, the time could be read off from a time disk graduated in hours and minutes. The nocturnal was replaced by the chronometer at sea, but was used until quite late in the eighteenth century.

4. HERO OF ALEXANDRIA
The exact period of Hero's work we do not know, but he belonged to the First Alexandrian School. We do know that he was an able mathematician. About 80 b.c., he put engineering and surveying on a more scientific basis. He is credited with the discovery of this formula for the area of a triangle where $s =$ half the sum of the sides of the triangle.

5. PENTACLE
The pentacle looks like two interlaced triangles. The pentacle and the pentagram are the same figure. It was used as a symbol of mystery by the Greeks, and various societies have used the symbol. In the Middle Ages, many people thought the pentacle had the power to keep away evil spirits.

6. PLANIMETER
This instrument is used for mechanically measuring the

area of an irregular plane figure. The hatchet planimeter is probably the simplest type and the wheel and disk, or Amsler type, is the most common.

7. FRUSTUM
Frustum means "a piece broken off." It refers to that portion of a regular solid left after cutting off the upper part by a plane parallel to the base, but it can also be used to describe the portion intercepted between any two planes.

8. APPROXIMATING AN AREA
The area is divided into any even number of parallel strips of equal breadth.

9. CUBE
A hexahedron is a solid figure which has six faces, so that the regular hexahedron is a cube, for it has six equal faces.

10. ELEVEN SECONDS
A "strike" occurs instantaneously and then there is a "rest" before the next strike. Hence, to strike six times requires five rests and this takes five seconds. There are eleven rests when the clock strikes "twelve."

12. Lighter Limericks

1. NOW

$$\text{Lunn's age} = 2 \times \text{son's age}$$
$$\text{or} \quad L = 2S$$
$$\text{and also} \quad (L - 25) = 3 \times (S - 25)$$
$$\text{or} \quad L = 3S - 75 + 25$$
$$\text{or} \quad 2S = 3S - 50$$
$$\text{or} \quad S = 50$$
$$\text{and} \quad L = 100$$

Thus we drink Grandpa's health just now—he is one hundred years old—a centenarian.

2. 42 *or* 21

This problem admits of two solutions, according to the way you interpret the wording of the limerick.

(a)
$$\frac{B - 1 + 3}{4} = 1 + 10$$

or $B + 2 = 44$

or $B = 42$

(b)
$$\frac{(B - 1) + (B + 3)}{4} = 1 + 10$$

or $2B + 2 = 44$

or $B = 21$

What a lucky young lady! More than enough boy friends for her to have a different one on each day of the month!

3. 5,000

Clive had in his hive one queen who laid the eggs and headed the colony, as many as 95,000 workers (daughters of the queen—undeveloped females), and only 5,000 drones (sons of the queen—fully developed males).

Workers + drones = 10^5 = 100,000

But 1 bee in every 20 bees was a drone

Number of drones $= \frac{1}{20} \times 100,000$

$= 5,000$

4. 4

Let H be the number of hits scored by Nero. Then, writing the information given in the form of an equation, we obtain:

$$H^2 - H - 12 = 0$$

$$\therefore \ (H - 4)(H + 3) = 0$$

$$\therefore \ H = 4 \ \text{ or } \ -3$$

Clearly the answer needed here is 4 but what is the significance of the -3?

5. 2 OUNCES

The solution of this problem is similar to that of the last one.

Let the weight of the ball be x ounces.

The equation obtained is another quadratic thus:

$$2x + x^2 - 8 = 0$$
$$\therefore \quad (x - 2)(x + 4) = 0$$
$$\therefore \quad x = 2 \quad \text{or} \quad -4$$

13. A Math Medley

1. CURSOR

The cursor is defined as a part of a mathematical instrument, which slides backwards and forwards. Newton suggested a cursor or runner should be used on a slide rule but his idea was not taken up for a hundred years. It is obvious when one is trying to read the graduations on two different scales that some convenient straight line is necessary, and the cursor is now an essential part of any slide rule.

2. MUSICAL SCALE

From our childhood we are accustomed to "do, re, mi, fa, sol, la, ti, do," which is known as the diatonic scale. Other scales are to be found in Turkish and Persian music! The frequencies of the eight notes of a diatonic scale are in the following ratio:

$\dfrac{1}{1} : \dfrac{9}{8} : \dfrac{5}{4} : \dfrac{4}{3} : \dfrac{3}{2} : \dfrac{5}{3} : \dfrac{15}{8} : \dfrac{2}{1}$, which is the same as

24 : 27 : 30 : 32 : 36 : 40 : 45 : 48, giving the notes
C   D   E   F   G   A   B   C′

3. 16.13 INCHES

In 60 minutes the tip of the minute hand of the clock makes one complete revolution tracing out the circumference of a circle whose radius is 7 inches.

In 60 minutes the tip moves through

$$\pi d \text{ inches} \quad \text{or} \quad \frac{22}{7} \times 2 \times 7 \text{ inches}$$

In 22 minutes the tip moves through

$$\frac{22}{7} \times 2 \times 7 \times \frac{22}{60} \text{ inches} \quad \text{or} \quad 16.13 \text{ inches}$$

4. CYCLOID

This is the simplest member of the class of curves known as roulettes. It was not known before the fifteenth century and not seriously studied until the seventeenth century. So many brilliant mathematicians like Descartes, Pascal, Leibnitz, the Bernoullis, and others have investigated the properties of the cycloid that it was sometimes named the "Helen of Geometers." It is a matter of opinion whether the curve, like Helen of Troy, is of surpassing beauty.

5. DESARGUES' ANSWER

OA, OB, and OC are three concurrent straight lines with X, Y, and Z any points on each respectively. Join CA and ZX and produce them to meet in R. Similarly, join AB and XY to meet in S, and CB and ZY to meet in T. Gérard Desargues, a seventeenth-century French engineer, proved that R, T, and S always lie on a straight line. Hence, if you plant your ten tulips in the positions of the ten points A, B, C, X, Y, Z, R, T, S, and O, they will be in ten rows of three.

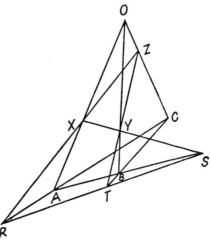

6. ABOUT THREE INCHES

The needle moves from the outermost groove to the innermost groove in an arc whose radius is the length of the pickup arm.

7. MR. PHILLIPS

Mr. Henry will earn during the first year $3,000.
Mr. Phillips will earn during the first year $1,500 + $1,500 + $300 = $3,300.
Mr. Henry will earn during the second year $3,000 + $600 = $3,600.
Mr. Phillips will earn during the second year $1,800 + $300 + $2,100 + $300 = $4,500.
Hence it is clear that Mr. Phillips will earn a sum of $1,200 more than Mr. Henry by the time they have both worked two years. As the years go by Mr. Phillips will earn increasingly more than Mr. Henry.

14. "C" Gets the Worst of It

1. $\frac{2}{15}$

The two relevant equations are: $B + C = \dfrac{2}{5}$

and $B = 2C$

From these we derive that $3C = \dfrac{2}{5}$ or $C = \dfrac{2}{15}$

2. $20\frac{20}{87}$ yards.

A runs 1,760 yards while B runs 1,740 yards and C runs 1,720 yards.

∴ B runs 1,740 yards while C runs 1,720 yards

$\therefore$ B runs 1,760 yards while C runs $\dfrac{1{,}720 \times 1{,}760}{1{,}740}$ yards

or $1{,}739\frac{67}{87}$ yards

$\therefore$ B beats C by $20\frac{20}{87}$ yards in a mile

3. 60 *DAYS*

$(A + B)$ do $\frac{1}{10}$ of the work in one day

$(A + C)$ do $\frac{1}{12}$ of the work in one day

$(B + C)$ do $\frac{1}{20}$ of the work in one day

Add these all together and we have:

$\therefore$ $2(A + B + C)$ do $\left(\frac{1}{10} + \frac{1}{12} + \frac{1}{20}\right)$ of the work in one day

or $(A + B + C)$ do $\frac{7}{60}$ of the work in one day

but $(A + B)$ do $\frac{1}{10}$ of the work in one day

$\therefore$ C alone does $\left(\frac{7}{60} - \frac{1}{10}\right)$ of the work in one day

or C alone does $\frac{1}{60}$ of the work in one day

$\therefore$ C can do all the work in sixty days

4. 18

A scores 50 while B scores 40

B scores 50 while C scores 40

$\therefore$ B scores 40 while C scores $\dfrac{40 \times 40}{50}$

or 32

$\therefore$ A scores 50 while B scores 40 and while C scores 32

$\therefore$ A can give 18 points to C

5. $500

The profit should be shared in the following proportions between A, B, and C: 1,875 : 1,500 : 1,250

or 15 : 12 : 10

or $\dfrac{15}{37}$: $\dfrac{12}{37}$: $\dfrac{10}{37}$

$\therefore$ C's share of the profit should be $\dfrac{\$10 \times 1{,}850}{37}$ or $500

6. $1\frac{11}{19}$ *HOURS*

In one hour A fills $\frac{1}{2}$, B fills $\frac{1}{3}$, and C empties $\frac{1}{5}$ of the tank.

∴ with all the pipes working $(\frac{1}{2} + \frac{1}{3} - \frac{1}{5})$ or $(\frac{19}{30})$ of the tank is filled in one hour

∴ with all the pipes working $\left(\dfrac{30}{30}\right)$ of the tank is filled in $\left(\dfrac{30}{19}\right)$ hours.

15. Letters for Numerals

1. $X = 9$, $Y = 1$, $Z = 8$

Examine the units column. $X + Y + Z = 10 + Z$, which means that $X + Y = 10$. Examine the tens column. $X + Y + Z + 1$ (from the units column) $= 10 + X$, which means that $Y + Z = 9$. Examine the ten-thousands column and the equation obtained is: $X + Y + Z + 1$ (from the thousands column) $= 10Y + X$. Substitute $Y + Z = 9$, and the equation then becomes: $10 = 10Y$, or $Y = 1$. From this it follows that $Z = 8$, and $X = 9$.

$$\begin{array}{r} 9999 \\ 1111 \\ 8888 \\ \hline 19998 \\ \hline \end{array}$$

2. $X = 5$, $N = 2$, $P = 1$, $S = 0$, $R = 6$, and $Z = 3$

Examine the second row of multiplication by X. X times X gives another X. ∴ X must be 0, or 1, or 5, or 6. $X \neq 0$ because the product is not XXX. $X \neq 1$ because the product is not PNX. $X \neq 6$ because there is no product of NX by X which will give ? NX. ∴ $X = 5$, because $25 \times 5 = 125$ or $75 \times 5 = 375$. ∴ $N = 2$ or 7. Examine the first row of multiplication by N. $N \neq 7$ because the product is not one of four figures. $\therefore$ N = 2. The remainder of the unknown letters follow fairly easily from this stage.

$$
\begin{array}{r}
125 \\
25 \\
\hline
625 \\
250 \\
\hline
3125 \\
\hline
\end{array}
$$

3. $P = 3, H = 1, I = 2, L = 5, T = 6$, and $S = 0$.

From the first division it is clear that H = 1. From the third division L times L gives another L in the units place. $\therefore$ L must be 0, or 1, or 5, or 6. L $\neq$ 0 because the product is not LL. L $\neq$ 1 because the product is not IL, and in any case H = 1. L $\neq$ 6 because whatever value is given to I, between 2 and 9, the product of 6 times I6 will not be 1I6. $\therefore$ L = 5. $\therefore$ HIL now reads 1I5. Examine the third division again. 5 times I5 is <200. $\therefore$ I must be 2 or 3. Examine the second division. In order to produce the product 5S, 2 times 25 would be possible and 3 times 35 impossible. $\therefore$ I = 2 and S = 0. The other letters are easily decoded from this stage.

$$
\begin{array}{r}
125 \\
25\overline{)3125} \\
25 \\
\hline
62 \\
50 \\
\hline
125 \\
125 \\
\hline
\cdots
\end{array}
$$

4. $A = 3, E = 9, F = 6, H = 0, L = 7, N = 1, P = 2$, and $Y = 5$

By a similar argument as in answer 3, Y must be 5 or 6. From the second subtraction in the units column $L - H = L$, $\therefore H = 0$. From the second division, in order to produce 0 in the units column, F must be even if $Y = 5$ and F must be 5 if $Y = 6$. From the second subtraction in the tens column $P - N = N$. $\therefore P = 2N$. $\therefore N \not> 4$, and P is even. From the first subtraction in the units column $L - Y = P$. As Y is 5 or 6 the only values P can have must be 2 or 4. $\therefore$ N must be 1 or 2. Now consider F and Y again, trying $F = 5$ and $Y = 6$ in the second division. An impossible result is obtained so that F must be even and $Y = 5$. Examine the first subtraction. $E - L = P$ and $L - Y = P$. By adding these $E - Y = 2P$. $\therefore E = 2P + 5$. $\therefore P = 2$. $\therefore L = 7$. This is the key and the remaining letters follow quickly.

$$
\begin{array}{r}
565 \\
35\overline{)19775} \\
175 \\
\hline
227 \\
210 \\
\hline
175 \\
175 \\
\hline
\cdots
\end{array}
$$

16. Some Short Stories

1. 1564. *WILLIAM SHAKESPEARE*
There are four digits in the year we are searching for in this story. Suppose we write the year as *ABCD*.
$A = 1$ because we have not yet reached the year 2000. Let us form equations from the facts given in the story:

$$
\begin{array}{rl}
A + D = B & \quad \ldots\ldots\ldots 1 \\
C = B + 1 & \quad \ldots\ldots 2 \\
3D = 2C & \quad \ldots\ldots\ldots 3
\end{array}
$$

Put in equation 3 a value for D in terms of B from equation 1 and at the same time put a value for C in terms of B from equation 2 and we have:

$$3(B - 1) = 2(B + 1)$$
$$\text{or} \quad B = 5$$
$$\text{Hence} \quad C = 6 \quad \text{and} \quad D = 4$$

Thus our gentleman was born in 1564. Who else could this be but William Shakespeare?

2. JULIETTE 16⅔, or 30 METERS, NEARER MONTREUX. LUCILE MISSES THE BUS EVERYWHERE

Draw your own diagram of a straight road and letter the position of the bus B, the point where the sisters left it P, the patch of narcissi where Juliette is J, and the correct meeting point with the bus for Juliette M.

Let us call the distance PM x meters.

Juliette runs MJ meters during the time the bus travels BM meters.

$$\therefore 2 \times MJ = 1 \times BM$$
$$\text{But} \quad MJ = \sqrt{40^2 + x^2} \quad \text{(Pythagoras)}$$
$$\text{and} \quad BM = 70 + x$$
$$\therefore \ 2\sqrt{40^2 + x^2} = 70 + x$$

$$\therefore \ 6{,}400 + 4x^2 = 4{,}900 + 140x + x^2$$
$$\therefore \ 3x^2 - 140x + 1{,}500 = 0$$
$$(3x - 50)(x - 30) = 0$$
$$x = 16\tfrac{2}{3}, \quad \text{or} \quad x = 30 \text{ meters}$$

Thus Juliette could have run to a point nearer Montreux by 16⅔, or 30 meters from the point where they left the road for the field, and she would have caught the bus.

Lucile was 41 meters from the road so her equation in the same way is:

$$2\sqrt{41^2 + x^2} = 70 + x$$

which becomes:

$$3x^2 - 140x + 1,824 = 0$$

and this equation will not give real roots like Juliette's equation. Thus poor sister Lucile missed the bus and wherever she had run she could never have caught it!

3. *TAKE MY CAMEL ALSO AND THEN DIVIDE*
When they included the camel belonging to the dervish there were eighteen camels in all. At first the eldest son took his share ($\frac{4}{9}$ of 18), that accounted for eight camels. The second son next took ($\frac{1}{3}$ of 18), or six camels, and finally the youngest one took his share, ($\frac{1}{6}$ of 18), that is three camels. To their surprise one camel was left over.
The dervish mounted the remaining camel, which happened to be his own, smiled and rode away waving friendly greetings.

4. *YES*
This is a Möbius band called after the German mathematician Möbius, who lived from 1790 to 1868. It is used in the modern branch of geometry called topology.

17. Brevity in Mathematics

1. *Q.E.D.*
This is the abbreviation for "Quod erat demonstrandum," a Latin phrase which can be translated as in the question. This dates back to the time when all mathematics books were written in Latin. In the geometry books today these letters appear at the end of each theorem. Placed at the end of each problem are the letters Q.E.F., standing for "Quod erat faciendum," which means "Which was to be done."

2. *cos θ*
All trigonometrical ratios of angles are abbreviated. These

are written sin θ, cos θ, tan θ, cosec θ, sec θ, cot θ. The cosine of an angle is the ratio of the base to the hypotenuse of the right-angled triangle. Some people remember these different ratios by means of this mnemonic "Some People Have Curly Brown Hair, Till Painted Black."

3. $f(x)$
As an example, $x^2 + 2x - 7$ depends for its value on the value given to x, and it is therefore called a function of x and is written $f(x)$. If $f(x) = 3x - 5$, and if x is given the value 3, then $f(3) = 3 \cdot 3 - 5 = 9 - 5 = 4$.

4. $\int 16x^3 dx$
$\int$ is called the operator and shows that the operation of integration is to take place on $16x^3$, and dx makes it clear that the integration is to be with respect to x. $\int 16x^3 dx = 4x^4$. If $4x^4$ were differentiated we should obtain $16x^3$. Integration and differentiation are two processes closely related to each other.

5. L.C.M.
This is the mathematical shorthand for "lowest common multiple." Thus the L.C.M. of 4, 8, and 12 is 24, because 24 is the smallest whole number into which 4, 8, and 12 will divide exactly.

6. *sinh x*
The functions $\frac{1}{2} (e^x - e^{-x})$ and $\frac{1}{2} (e^x + e^{-x})$ possess properties analogous to sin x and cos x. These functions are therefore defined as "hyperbolic sine" and "hyperbolic cosine" of x. Sinh $x = \frac{1}{2} (e^x - e^{-x})$, and cosh $x = \frac{1}{2} (e^x + e^{-x})$. Just as $\sin^2 x + \cos^2 x = 1$, so $\cosh^2 x - \sinh^2 x = 1$.

7. i
If $x^2 = -1$, then we can find no real number to satisfy the equation. The Swiss mathematician, Euler, introduced the symbol i for $\sqrt{-1}$. The symbol is used when dealing with "complex numbers." It is also essential when studying both the theory of air-flow patterns and alternating currents.

68

8. G.C.D.

This is the abbreviation for "greatest common divisor." Thus 3 is the G.C.D. of 6, 9, and 12. It is usual to find the G.C.D. by writing down the prime factors of each number and noting those that are common to all.

9. $\dfrac{dy}{dx}$

This is the differential coefficient of y with respect to x, or the first derivative of y with respect to x. It can also be considered to be the gradient of the tangent to the graph of y plotted against x. If $\dfrac{dy}{dx}$ is constant at different points along the graph, then the graph is a straight line; if $\dfrac{dy}{dx}$ varies, then the graph is a curve.

10. e

The eccentricity of a conic is the ratio between the distance of a point on the curve from the focus and the distance of the same point from the directrix. The following values for e are always true: $e < 1$ for the ellipse, $e = 1$ for the parabola, and $e > 1$ for the hyperbola.

18. Was Charlie Coping?

1. *RIGHT*

The answer is not correct according to Charlie's way of thinking—merely to reverse all the numbers is not the correct way.

2. *RIGHT*

Again it is the right answer but the wrong way. Will it happen once more?

3. *RIGHT*

$$\sqrt{5\tfrac{5}{24}} = \sqrt{\tfrac{125}{24}} = \sqrt{\tfrac{25 \cdot 5}{24}} = 5\sqrt{\tfrac{5}{24}}$$

4. *RIGHT*

$$\sqrt[3]{2\tfrac{2}{7}} = \sqrt[3]{\tfrac{16}{7}} = \sqrt[3]{\tfrac{8 \cdot 2}{7}} = 2\sqrt[3]{\tfrac{2}{7}}$$

5. *RIGHT*

Charlie is correct this time but does he realize why this is so? His conclusion does not necessarily follow from the first part of the question. He does not use the word "therefore" correctly.

6. *RIGHT*

He succeeds in obtaining the answer, but $\sin(a + b)$ does not equal $\sin a + \sin b$! In fact $\sin(a + b) \cdot \sin(a - b)$ should be $\sin^2 a \cdot \cos^2 b - \cos^2 a \cdot \sin^2 b$, and the solution follows from here.

7. *RIGHT*

You will notice that you are given two equations to find two unknowns, and Charlie uses only one of them. Also he writes in error that $\dfrac{x - 1}{y} = \dfrac{x}{y} - 1$. Finally, although $\dfrac{x}{y} = \dfrac{5}{6}$, it does not follow that $x = 5$, and $y = 6$; there are many other possibilities!

8. *RIGHT*

No working is necessary here—just count the number of triangles.

Although Charlie's work shows consistently correct answers, there is an amazingly incorrect use of "therefore" in writing and by symbol! In the first four examples, it is essential to show the working. Perhaps he has worked his examples properly on a piece of scrap paper, or perhaps he has just guessed.

19. Can You Arrange These?

1. 120

This is an illustration of the multiplicative principle. In this case there are twelve ways of choosing the boy for president. With each of these ways it is possible to choose the girl for vice-president in ten ways. The particular girl who is chosen is not determined by the choice of the boy. The choice of each is made independently and in succession, so that the total number of possibilities is the product of the two possibilities.

2. 720

This may seem a big number of arrangements. It is the product of $6 \times 5 \times 4 \times 3 \times 2 \times 1$. Another way of writing this product is $\lfloor 6$, or, as it is often printed, 6!. It is called factorial 6. In this example, the left-hand boy can be any one of them, so there are six ways of choosing him. The next boy from the left-hand side can be chosen in five ways from the remaining five boys. The next boy in four ways, the next boy in three ways, and so on. If there were eight boys altogether (only two more), the number of possible arrangements would be 8! or 40,320. If there were ten boys, then there would be more than three million ways of arranging them.

3. 120

This is not the same answer as in the last question because it is only the order which is considered and not the actual position. There will be six positions in which the same order will be found but each position will be turned around relatively to the other. Another way of considering this problem is to keep one boy always in the same place and then arrange the remaining five boys. This can be done in 5! ways, or 120. Any order arranged clockwise has an equivalent order arranged counterclockwise. The number of 120 different ways includes both these as separate arrangements. It is considered that sitting on a person's right is different from sitting on his left. These two arrangements are mirror images of one another.

4. $26 \times 25 \times 24 = 15{,}600$

This is called a "permutation of 26 different letters taken 3 at a time" and is written in mathematical language as $_{26}P_3$. It is fairly easy to see how one arrives at this calculation. Expressed in terms of factorials, it is the result of dividing factorial 26 by factorial $(26 - 3)$. In general the number of permutations of n things if only r are taken at any one time is $_nP_r$ or factorial n divided by factorial $(n - r)$.

5. $3 \times 3 \times 3 \times 3 = 3^4 = 81$

Consider each game separately. The first game may be won, lost, or drawn by one of the teams. Therefore there are three possibilities in this result. For each one of these first-game possibilities the second game has three possibilities. This makes nine possible forecasts for the first two games. For each of these nine forecasts the third game has three possibilities and so on. Hence for four games there are 81 different forecasts possible. If you are absolutely certain of the result of one of these games, then you need only make $3 \times 3 \times 3$ or 27 forecasts to ensure that among them is one complete correct forecast. If you can "bank" on two results, then you need only make 3×3 or 9 forecasts to ensure you have one correct forecast of all the four games.

6. 36

The argument is the same as in the last question. The first die may fall in six different ways and with each of these ways there are six possibilities for the second die. The total scores range from 2 to 12.

7. 1,728

What difficulty the captain will have in deciding the order of rowing in the boat for his crew if he has so many possibilities! This number 1,728 can be obtained in several ways. Consider the stroke-side men first: the fourth oarsman can be chosen from the three who can row on either side in three ways; when this fourth oarsman is chosen, the four stroke-side oarsmen can be arranged in 4! ways; therefore there are

3 × 4! ways of arranging the stroke side. Now consider the bow-side oarsmen. There is no choice of men. There are two bow-side oarsmen and two who can row on either side. These can be arranged in 4! ways. For each stroke-side arrangement any one of the bow-side arrangements is possible. Thus the total number of arrangements is 3 × 4! × 4!, which is 1,728.

20. Puzzle These Out

1. 39 DAYS
During the last and fortieth day the pond which was half covered becomes completely covered—just doubled in one day!

2. 2 GALLONS
A volume has three dimensions and each is doubled according to the question. Hence the new volume is 2 × 2 × 2 times the original volume.

3. PHILADELPHIA
The train leaving Atlantic City travels the faster, so naturally they meet and cross one another nearer to Philadelphia. In fact, the meeting place is $\frac{4}{90}$ of 60, or $26\frac{2}{3}$ miles from Philadelphia, and $\frac{5}{90}$ of 60, or $33\frac{1}{3}$ miles from Atlantic City, and this happens at 10:40 A.M.

4. (a) 15, (b) 7, (c) 21
(a) The numbers in this series double themselves for each new term.
(b) These numbers are the cubes of the natural numbers.
(c) Each number in this series is five greater than the previous number.

5. (a) 9, (b) 16, (c) 20
(a) Each term in this series is one third of the previous term.
(b) These numbers are the squares of the natural numbers.
(c) These numbers are 1 × 2, 2 × 3, 3 × 4, 4 × 5, 5 × 6, . . .

6. GREATEST: LOG 2 + LOG 4,
LEAST: LOG 6 − LOG 3

$\log (2 + 4) \quad = \log 6$
$\log 2 + \log 4 = \log (2 \times 4) = \log 8$
$\log (6 - 3) \quad = \log 3$
$\log 6 - \log 3 = \log (6 \div 3) = \log 2$
Log 8 is the greatest and log 2 is the smallest of these values.

7. I, II, III, IIII, V, VI
The usual way of writing "four" in Roman numerals is IV.

21. Browsing in Books

1. AN AID FOR READING A NUMBER
Tonstall, who became Bishop of London during the early part of the sixteenth century, gave some interesting information about the "new" Hindu-Arabic number system and arithmetic in England. In his book *De Arte Supputandi* he shows place value by means of dots or points above the figures. We have become used to commas being placed in such a way as to group the figures in threes. Hence 567342452 is now written as 567,342,452.

2. PREPARATION TO FIND THE SQUARE ROOT
Tonstall in his arithmetic book includes a method of finding the square root of a number. Just as we mark off in pairs from the decimal point, he does the same thing but shows it by means of the superior point placed over the first figure in each group. Thus 98525476 is the same as $\overline{98}\,\overline{52}\,\overline{54}\,\overline{76}$ or as 98′52′54′76.

3. MULTIPLICATION OF 9 BY 6
Robert Recorde's arithmetic book *The Grounde of Artes* was the arithmetic book of the century 1543-1643. In this book he gives the rule for multiplying 6 by 6 up to 9 by 9. In the

74

question we have to multiply 9 by 6. A large cross is drawn and the 9 and the 6 are written on the left-hand side. Subtract each from 10 to give 1 and 4 respectively. Now multiply the two differences together, 1 by 4 = 4 and this is the units figure in the answer. Subtract either the 4 from the 9 or 1 from the 6 (that is why the cross is drawn) and then we have the tens figure which is 5. So the answer is 54. We wonder if it isn't easier to learn your tables.

4. *DIVISION BY* 10
Recorde suggested a vertical line to show the division when a number was divided by ten.

5. *DIVISION OF VULGAR FRACTIONS*
Another process shown by Recorde is the multiplication and division of fractions. In division, which we choose in this question, there is no rule about turning the divisor upside down and multiplying. The division is carried out by cross-multiplying. Cross-multiply the 1 and 4 for the numerator and the 3 and 3 for the denominator.

6. *WRITING A DECIMAL*
83 4′ 2″ 5‴ is the same as 83.425. A commercial arithmetic was published by Francesco Pellos in Turin in 1492, and in it he unwittingly used the familiar decimal point. Later writers, however, used a bar to represent the decimal point. John Napier, the inventor of logarithms, used the style as in the question but later changed this. There must have been at least a dozen methods of writing decimals and today 23·45; 23.45; and 23,45 are used in different countries.

7. *MULTIPLICATION TO FIND AN AREA*
This example is taken from John Bonnycastle's book *The Scholar's Guide to Arithmetic,* which was published in 1780. The first line of multiplication is done by 5 feet and the second line by 4 inches. In 1780 the answer would have been given as 19 square feet, 6⅔ square inches. This is wrong. It should read "19 square feet, 6 'feet-inches,' and 8

square inches," and this makes 19 square feet and 80 square inches—the correct answer. It is the same as the area of a strip 1 foot wide and 19 feet, $6\frac{2}{3}$ inches long.

8. RULE OF THREE or PROPORTION

If five books cost 25 dollars, what will eight books cost? The 5 and the 8 being of the same kind (books) are placed on the same side, and the 25 dollars is placed opposite the 5 because they are linked together. The rule as stated by Recorde is to multiply 8 by 25 and divide by 5 and hence the cross line!

22. Strange Figures Formed by Figures

1. 1 6 15 20 15 6 1

These numbers are obtained by adding together the figures found on the left hand and the right hand immediately above the dashes.

2. 9 36 84 126 126 84 36 9

The extreme numbers on either side of the line are both 1. The other numbers are obtained as explained in the answer to question number 1. In exactly the same way, line after line can be added indefinitely to the triangle.

3. THIRD AND FOURTH LINES

The full expansions are:

$(x + a)^2 = 1(x^2) + 2(ax) + 1(a^2)$
$(x + a)^3 = 1(x^3) + 3(ax^2) + 3(a^2x) + 1(a^3)$

The numbers or the coefficients of the terms in this type of expansion are readily obtained by the direct application of the binomial theorem which states that:

$$(x + a)^n = x^n + nx^{n-1}a + \frac{n(n-1)}{1 \cdot 2}x^{n-2}a^2 +$$

$$\frac{n(n-1)(n-2)}{1 \cdot 2 \cdot 3}x^{n-3}a^3 + \text{etc., etc.}$$

4. 1 8 24 32 16

The numbers in the fifth line of the triangle are 1, 4, 6, 4, 1.
∴ the expansion of $(x + 2)^4 = x^4 + 4(x^3 2) + 6(x^2 2^2) + 4(x 2^3) + 2^4$. From this the coefficients as above are derived. Both the coefficients and the actual terms are found by substituting $a = 2$ and $n = 4$ in the binomial expansion stated in the last answer thus:

$$(x + 2)^4 = x^4 + 4x^3 2 + \frac{4 \cdot 3}{1 \cdot 2} x^2 2^2 + \frac{4 \cdot 3 \cdot 2}{1 \cdot 2 \cdot 3} x 2^3 +$$

$$\frac{4 \cdot 3 \cdot 2 \cdot 1}{1 \cdot 2 \cdot 3 \cdot 4} x^0 2^4$$

$$\therefore (x + 2)^4 = x^4 + 8x^3 + 24x^2 + 32x + 16$$

5. PASCAL

Pascal contributed much to mathematics, including a paper on the arithmetical triangle. Hence the name "Pascal's triangle." Other mathematicians—Tartaglia (1560), Schenbel (1558), and Bienewitz (1524)—had used this to determine the coefficients in a binomial expansion, but they had not dealt with the arrangement as thoroughly as Pascal did in his *Traité du triangle arithmétique,* printed in 1654.

6. 15. MAGIC SQUARE

A magic square is an arrangement of numbers such that the sum in each row, each column, and each diagonal is the same. The earliest magic square dates back to about 2200 B.C., and no doubt it was familiar to the Chinese then. The squares were arranged in "orders," and one can appreciate why magic properties, such as longevity and disease prevention, became associated with these squares.

7.

16	2	12
6	10	14
8	18	4

To obtain the missing numbers, first find the total of the top row or the left-hand column. This equals 30. Then calculate the center number from the diagonal. The rest follow easily from this point.

8.

1	15	14	4
12	6	7	9
8	10	11	5
13	3	2	16

This is a magic square using all the numbers 1 to 16 only. It is formed from a basic square in which all these numbers are included written in order left to right across each row in turn. All the numbers cut by both diagonals are retained but all the others are interchanged with their diametrically opposite numbers.

23. Fun with Problems

1. 1, 1·2, 1·2·3, 1·2·3·4, 1·2·3·4·5, ...
Each term in this series is a factorial, which means the product of all the numbers from 1 to the particular term considered. The first five terms of this series are thus: 1, 2, 6, 24, 120, and the sum of these is 153.

2. *HERE THEY ARE:*

$$\frac{2}{4} = \frac{3}{6} = \frac{79}{158}, \qquad \frac{3}{6} = \frac{9}{18} = \frac{27}{54}, \qquad \frac{2}{6} = \frac{3}{9} = \frac{58}{174}$$

3. *1 POUND, 3 POUNDS, 9 POUNDS*
The key to this is that the boy can put any combination of weights on either pan and the difference between the two weights is the amount of fruit he sells. Thus the weight he requires is the result of an addition or subtraction sum.

$1 - 0 = 1$, $3 - 1 = 2$, $3 - 0 = 3$, $(3 + 1) - 0 = 4$, $9 - (3 + 1) = 5$, $9 - 3 = 6$, $(9 + 1) - 3 = 7$, $9 - 1 = 8$, $9 - 0 = 9$, $(9 + 1) - 0 = 10$, $(9 + 3) - 1 = 11$, $(9 + 3) - 0 = 12$, and finally $(9 + 3 + 1) - 0 = 13$.

4. *YES*

$$\frac{9}{\sqrt{9} \times \sqrt{9}}, \qquad \frac{9}{9} + \sqrt{9}, \qquad \frac{9}{\sqrt{9}} + \sqrt{9}$$

5. NORTH POLE

Yes, and there are other places too! These places lie on a parallel of latitude in the Southern Hemisphere 100 miles north of a parallel of latitude that has a total length of 100 miles. Can you puzzle this out?

6.   264 feet, 880 yards

60 miles per hour = 88 feet per second

∴ length of train   = 88 × 3 feet

= 264 feet

To pass completely through the tunnel, the train must travel for a time of thirty seconds.

∴ length of tunnel   = 88 × 30 feet

= 880 yards

24. Tackle These Twisters

1. HARMONIC PROGRESSION

This is sometimes abbreviated to H.P., but don't confuse it with a horse! If a, b, and c are in harmonic progression, then $\frac{1}{a}$, $\frac{1}{b}$, and $\frac{1}{c}$ are in arithmetical progression. Thus 1, $\frac{1}{2}$, $\frac{1}{3}$, $\frac{1}{4}$ . . . form a harmonic progression, for 1, 2, 3, 4 . . . are in arithmetical progression. In music strings of the same material with the same diameter and tension, but with lengths in harmonic progression, produce harmonic tones.

2. FIBONACCI SERIES

This series consists of the numbers 0, 1, 1, 2, 3, 5, 8, 13, 21, . . . The sum of the second and third terms equals the fourth term, and the sum of the third and fourth terms equals the fifth term, and so on all the way through the series. This series is named after Fibonacci, who is generally known as Leonardo of Pisa. He was born in 1175. Curiously, the leaves on a stalk, the petals of some flowers, and lettuce leaves follow the ratios of successive terms of the Fibonacci series.

3. LET US SEE!

$$S = 1 + 3x + 5x^2 + \ldots\ldots\ldots + 39x^{19}$$
$$Sx = \quad\quad x + 3x^2 + \ldots\ldots\ldots + 37x^{19} + 39x^{20}$$

By subtraction:

$$S(1 - x) = 1 + 2x + 2x^2 + \ldots\ldots\ldots + 2x^{19} - 39x^{20}$$
$$= 1 + \frac{2x(1 - x^{19})}{1 - x} - 39x^{20}$$
$$= \frac{1 - x + 2x - 2x^{20} - 39x^{20} + 39x^{21}}{1 - x}$$
$$\text{Sum} = \frac{39x^{21} - 41x^{20} + x + 1}{(1 - x)^2}$$

4. (a) 19·21·23   (b) 28,560

In order to find the sum of n terms of this series, write down the last term multiplied by the next highest factor and subtract the first term multiplied by the next lowest factor, and then divide by the product of (the number of factors in each term + 1) and (the common difference of the factors). Obeying these instructions in this particular series we get:

$$\text{Sum} = \frac{19·21·23·25 - 3·5·7·9}{(3 + 1)·2}$$
$$= \frac{229,425 - 945}{8}$$
$$= 28,560$$

5. NO

At first sight this may appear strange, but if we put $x = 1$ in this series we obtain:

$$\log_e 2 = 1 - \frac{1}{2} + \frac{1}{3} - \frac{1}{4} + \frac{1}{5} - \ldots\ldots\ldots$$

In order to get the value of the logarithm correct to four places of decimals, we should have to consider hundreds of terms of this series. Life is too short for this! Fortunately other series can be deduced from $\log_e (1 + x)$ which are more quickly convergent and hence more useful for the calculation of logarithms.

80

6. Sin x

Both sin x and cos x are functions of x and they can both be expanded in a series of terms which are in ascending powers of x. Using Maclaurin's theorem, it is a simple matter to show that

$$\sin x = x - \frac{x^3}{3!} + \frac{x^5}{5!} - \frac{x^7}{7!} + \ldots\ldots\ldots$$

x in these expansions is measured in radians and not degrees. (π radians $= 180°$). Using this series we can soon work out the value of various sines. For instance, if we put $x = 0.2$ in the series we shall find that sin x has a value of 0.1988. Now convert x from radian measure into degrees:

$$x = \frac{0.2 \times 180}{3.14} \text{ degrees}$$
$$= 11°28'$$

Thus we succeed in calculating that sin $11°\ 28' = 0.1988$.

7. EXPONENTIAL

The base of natural logarithms is e, and this quantity is the sum to infinity of the series:

$$1 + \frac{1}{1!} + \frac{1}{2!} + \frac{1}{3!} + \frac{1}{4!} + \ldots\ldots\ldots\ldots$$

The peculiarity of this series is that when it is raised to the power x the following series is obtained:

$$1 + \frac{x}{1!} + \frac{x^2}{2!} + \frac{x^3}{3!} + \frac{x^4}{4!} + \ldots\ldots\ldots\ldots$$

and this series is convergent for all finite values of x. This series, which is the expansion of e^x, is known as the exponential series.

25. Some Statistical Studies

1. HISTOGRAM

Let us suppose that we know the heights of a thousand men

picked at random. Tabulate the number of men whose heights lie in the equal ranges between 64 and 65 inches, 65 and 66 inches, 66 and 67 inches, and so on. Plot on a graph the frequency (number of men) in each range against the heights by making a series of columns whose areas are proportional to the frequency. This is a histogram and the diagram above the questions is one such graph.

2. FREQUENCY POLYGON
On the histogram mark the mid-points of all the ranges of the variable quantity as shown in the same diagram. Join these mid-points by a jagged line. This is a frequency polygon. When the number of observations is increased considerably, this frequency polygon becomes a frequency curve. This is made possible by choosing smaller ranges of the variable quantity and at the same time having a large number of observations in each range.

3. NORMAL CURVE
Many variable quantities form this shape of curve as their frequency curve. Some examples are: heights of persons, sizes of shoes worn by people, and intelligence quotients. One of the characteristics of this normal curve is that it is always smooth and symmetrical.

4. MEAN
This is what the ordinary person means when he speaks of an average. It is the "average" of everyday life. It is obtained by adding together all the values of the variable quantity and then dividing this by the total number of these values. In this way we should find, for instance, the average consumption of milk per person per day, or the average life span of a horse. Do batting averages work out in this way? What about the batters not out?

5. MODE
This is an average often used in statistics. It is the most commonly occurring value in a series of observations of a variable quantity. In a symmetrical frequency curve (or normal curve), the mean and the mode are the same. In the lopsided curve or skew curve, they are different.

6. STANDARD DEVIATION

Sometimes the observed values of a variable quantity are all close to the mean value. Sometimes they are widely dispersed. The standard deviation tells us the degree to which they are dispersed. This standard deviation, denoted by the Greek letter sigma, σ, is calculated by taking the square root of the arithmetic mean of the squares of the deviations from the mean. Mean error, mean square error, and error of mean square are other names for standard deviation. σ^2 is called the variance.

7. RANDOM

The words "random sample" abbreviate the phrase "a sample chosen in a random way." This type of sampling is often carried out by making use of a table of random numbers. After numbering the items in a population, it is then a simple matter to select those items or samples by consulting the table. This is done to prevent personal bias. Such sampling is obviously necessary for a dealer buying apples, a metallurgist in testing material, a manufacturer of electric-light bulbs, etc. Random sampling saves time and energy.

26. A Few Fast Ones

1. HALFWAY

If you go farther you are coming out again and nearer the edge!

2. EVERY FOUR MINUTES

The buses are evenly spaced along the highway in both directions. He counts every hour twenty moving in one direction and ten in the opposite direction. There are thirty buses in that section over which he travels in an hour, and half of these buses turn around in the hour. Therefore fifteen must leave the terminus every hour or one bus every four minutes.

3. TWELVE

4. 400 π FEET

Subtract the circumference of the earth 2π (4,000 miles) from the circumference flown by the airplane 2π (4,000 miles + 200 feet). The difference is 2π 200 feet.

5. 20,000

Assuming also that one man has one wife, then:

$$\frac{42}{100} \text{ of the males} = \frac{28}{100} \text{ of the females}$$

or $42M = 28F$
or $M : F = 28 : 42$
or $M : F = 2 : 3$

Therefore two-fifths of the population is male, or there are 20,000 males.

6. YOU WILL NOT BE ABLE TO HOP OUT

You hop 4½ feet at the first attempt, which is halfway out, and then another 2¼ feet at the next hop. Thus you are already three quarters of the way out in two hops. You feel encouraged, for surely the last quarter will be hopped easily! Let us write down the hops:

$4\frac{1}{2}$, $2\frac{1}{4}$, $1\frac{1}{8}$, $\frac{9}{16}$, $\frac{9}{32}$, $\frac{9}{64}$, $\frac{9}{128}$, $\frac{9}{256}$, $\frac{9}{512}$, $\frac{9}{1024}$, and so on.

Add these up and you will see that you are nearly there—in fact, you can hop more than 8¾ feet of the total distance needed of 9 feet. But this is a series whose "sum to infinity" is less than 9 feet. You are a prisoner in the circle!

7. YES

The first box could contain $(x + 1)$ or $(x + 2)$ pieces of candy and the second box could contain $(y + 1)$ or $(y + 2)$ pieces, where both x and y separately are divisible by three. Then neither of the two boxes alone could contain a number of candies divisible by three.

There are four possible ways in which these boxes can be filled with candy, and they are:

$$(x + 1) \quad \text{and} \quad (y + 1)$$
$$(x + 2) \quad \text{and} \quad (y + 1)$$
$$(x + 2) \quad \text{and} \quad (y + 2)$$
$$(x + 1) \quad \text{and} \quad (y + 2)$$

The other point noted by the student is that the second box has seven more pieces than the first box, which can be expressed in these four ways:

$(y + 1) - (x + 1) = 7$ or $y - x = 7$, which is impossible.
$(y + 1) - (x + 2) = 7$ or $y - x = 8$, which is impossible.
$(y + 2) - (x + 2) = 7$ or $y - x = 7$, which is impossible.
$(y + 2) - (x + 1) = 7$ or $y - x = 6$, which is possible because six is divisible by three.

Thus it is possible to fill the two boxes with candy in such a way that the conditions of the question are fulfilled. In fact, if we remember that y is always six greater than x, and that x is always a multiple of three, then we can calculate pairs of values for $(x + 1)$ and $(y + 2)$.

Here are some ways that the two boxes can be filled with candy:

First box	...	1	and	second box	...	8
	...	4			...	11
	...	7			...	14
	...	10			...	17
	...	13			...	20

27. Calculus Cocktails

1. 1½ MILES

Suppose the hiker strikes the road at X, a distance of x miles from P. Let T be the total time taken by the hiker to reach the inn. It is the time that has to be a minimum to fulfill the conditions of the question.

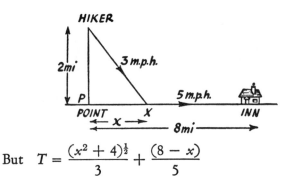

But $T = \dfrac{(x^2 + 4)^{\frac{1}{2}}}{3} + \dfrac{(8 - x)}{5}$

Differentiate T with respect to the variable x:

$$\frac{dT}{dx} = \frac{1}{3} \cdot \frac{1}{2} \cdot \frac{2x}{(x^2 + 4)^{\frac{1}{2}}} - \frac{1}{5}$$

There is a "minimum" when:

$$\frac{x}{3(x^2 + 4)^{\frac{1}{2}}} = \frac{1}{5}$$

$$\text{or when} \quad 5x = 3(x^2 + 4)^{\frac{1}{2}}$$
$$\text{or when} \quad x = 1\tfrac{1}{2} \text{ miles.}$$

2. 96 π CUBIC INCHES

The section of the space hat is a parabola of the form $y^2 = 4ax$. Substitute one set of known values of the space hat and we have:

$$y^2 = 4ax$$
$$\text{or} \quad 4^2 = 4a \cdot 12$$

$$\therefore \ a = \frac{1}{3}$$

The equation of the parabola is $3y^2 = 4x$.

By integration we have the volume of the hat thus:

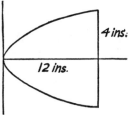

$$\text{Volume} = \pi \int_0^{12} \frac{4}{3} \cdot x \cdot dx$$

$$= \pi \left[\frac{4}{3} \cdot \frac{x^2}{2} \right]_0^{12} \text{ cubic inches}$$

$\therefore$ <u>Volume $= 96\,\pi$ cubic inches</u>

3. 1,152 CUBIC INCHES

Let V be the volume of the box.
Let x be the side of the squares cut out.
Then $V = (32 - 2x)(20 - 2x)x$
   or $V = 640x - 104x^2 + 4x^3$
$\therefore \dfrac{dV}{dx} = 640 - 208x + 12x^2$

For a maximum volume, $\dfrac{dV}{dx} = 0$

   or $3x^2 - 52x + 160 = 0$
   or $(3x - 40)(x - 4) = 0$
   or $x = 4$ or $x = \dfrac{40}{3}$

Using the real value of $x = 4$, the maximum volume of the box is $24 \times 12 \times 4 = 1,152$ cubic inches.

4. 573 FEET

Consider a small angular movement $d\theta$ takes place during a small displacement ds. Then if R is the radius of the circle in which it moves:

$$\frac{1}{R} = \frac{d\theta}{ds}$$

$$\therefore\ ds = R\,d\theta$$

$$\therefore\ s = R\int_{0}^{\frac{\pi}{6}} d\theta = R\left[\theta\right]_{0}^{\frac{\pi}{6}}$$

$$\therefore \ 2 \cdot 150 = R \cdot \frac{\pi}{6}$$

$$\therefore \ \underline{R = 573 \text{ feet}}$$

28. Track the Term

1. CIRCLE
The use of the phrase "circle of influence" seems to go back as far as the late seventeenth century. Later it seems that it was considered that either a person or an object exerted its influence on all planes and hence the phrase "sphere of influence." We should also note the use of the word "circle" with reference to a group of persons surrounding a center of interest. What is the family circle?

2. SQUARE
To the golfer who has been trailing against an opponent for nearly a complete round, the words "all square" will come as sweet music. The word "square" was used in the sixteenth century to mean concur, correspond, or agree with. In 1887 golfers began using the term with reference to equal scores.

3. ZERO
It is from the zero mark on a graduated scale that reckoning begins. Hence we can see how the military term "zero hour" came into being. It means the precise time at which an operation or attack is planned to begin. It became a term in general use in the first World War and has filtered through into our more sensible and civilian life with the same meaning. All students face a zero hour with their examinations!

4. DIVIDE
We, in America, all know the particular use of this word to mean a ridge or line of high ground forming the division between two river valleys or systems—a watershed. "The Great Divide."

5. PROPORTION

The phrase intended here is "out of all proportion." How often do we consider a punishment to be out of all proportion or excessive for the particular offense committed? Proportion in the mathematical sense is an exact equality of ratios.

6. QUOTIENT

In mathematics the quotient is obtained by dividing one quantity by another. In order to have a unit for intelligence, it has been found that the most useful is that obtained by dividing the mental age by the chronological age and multiplying the result by 100. This quantity is called the I.Q. or "intelligence quotient." We hope yours is over 100!

7. PENTAGON

It is on record that in 1571 a fort with five bastions was called a pentagon. Thus the use of a "Pentagon Building" for a military establishment has a precedent in history. In mathematics a plane rectilinear figure having five sides and having five angles is called a pentagon. In the regular pentagon the five sides are equal.

8. EXPONENT

In algebra the word "exponent" is used to describe the symbol denoting a power and it is sometimes called an index. In everyday use "exponent" is used of one who expounds or interprets.

9. NEGATIVE

In the seventeenth century "negative" was first employed to denote quantities to be subtracted from other quantities, but the sign we use for this operation did not become popular until some years later. The term is in general use, of course, with reference to rejection and the veto.

10. SUMS

A judge "sums" up the evidence or recapitulates briefly the facts proven during the trial. A "sum" in mathematics is the result obtained by addition or, more loosely, refers to a problem in arithmetic.

29. Arches

1. OGEE

The ogee arch is constructed as in the diagram. This type of arch became especially popular in the fourteenth century in Italy, but owing to its weakness it could only be used in the windows of a church. The points C in this and the other diagrams represent the centers of curvature of sections of the arch.

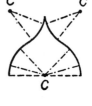

2. LANCET

The lancet arch is composed of two arcs. The centers of these arcs are situated on the springing line produced and outside the arch itself. Lancet windows were popular in the early thirteenth century when two or more of them were placed close together to secure as much light as possible.

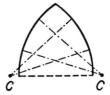

3. MOORISH

This is a pointed arch consisting of two arcs but it differs from the lancet type in that the centers for describing the arcs lie within the opening of the arch itself. This architectural feature appeared for the first time in the ninth century in a mosque in Cairo, and soon became an emblem of the Mohammedan faith. The Moors in Northwest Africa did not use it.

4. RAMPANT

The rampant arch has, as a special feature, springing points at different levels, but this is essential because the arch is used to support a flight of steps that may be solid.

5. EQUILATERAL

This type is constructed on an equilateral triangle, as in the diagram. This arch was popular in the late thirteenth century, and you will notice that it is much wider than the lancet type. This arch is sometimes called the Early English or pointed arch.

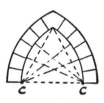

6. SEGMENTAL

As its name implies, the segmental arch is formed from the segment of a circle. The Romans are really responsible for the introduction of arched construction work. In the segmental arch we have a wonderful example of how bricks can be arranged in a curved structure so that they give mutual support to one another.

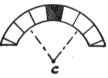

7. HORSESHOE

The arc of the horseshoe arch is greater than a semicircle, with its center above the springing line of the arch. This arch was widely employed in Moorish architecture. It was the horseshoe arch that the Moors brought into Spain, where they built, among other things, the Great Mosque at Cordova. The arch was copied by the French in the south, and ultimately a few doorways and windows were decorated by it in England toward the end of the twelfth century.

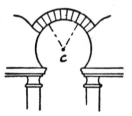

8. FOUR-CENTERED (TUDOR)

This arch was first made in the building revival that came with the Tudors and so it is sometimes called the Tudor arch. It is formed by using the arcs of four circles, and is a much stronger and wider arch than the ogee arch. The builders of churches of this period had to provide large east windows so that the four-centered arch was the perfect answer.

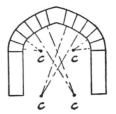

9. NORMAN

The so-called Norman period dates from 1066 to 1189. The Normans were great builders, and after the conquest of Britain many church buildings were erected there. It is a common mistake to think that a semicircular arch in a church is necessarily of Norman construction. The pillars, moldings, or ornamentations must be examined. The plain zigzag ornamentation called the chevron is frequently found on the Norman arch. Saxon arches were semicircular but their moldings, if present, were very plain.

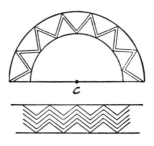

30. Circles, Circles & More Circles

1. DIRECTOR

The locus of the intersection of pairs of perpendicular tangents to an ellipse is a circle, and this circle is called the director circle of the ellipse.

2. AUXILIARY

The circle which is described with the major axis of the ellipse as diameter is called the auxiliary circle of the ellipse.

Unlike the director circle, the auxiliary circle will touch the ellipse in two points at the extremities of the longer or major axis. Draw a circle, and from a number of points on it drop perpendiculars on a diameter. Divide these perpendiculars in a given ratio (say 2:3). The join of these points will form an ellipse with the original circle as the auxiliary circle.

3. NINE-POINT

This circle as its name suggests passes through nine points. Six of these points are mentioned in the question and the remaining three are "the mid-points of the lines between the vertices and the common point of intersection of the altitudes."

4. ORTHOGONAL

Orthogonal means "right-angled; pertaining to or depending upon the use of right angles." If any two curves cut at right angles, they are said to intersect orthogonally. Such curves are of interest in many branches of applied mathematics. One point of interest about two circles cutting orthogonally is that the square of the distance between the centers is equal to the sum of the squares of their radii.

5. INSCRIBED

A circle is said to be inscribed in a polygon when each side is tangential to the circle. Consider the case of the simplest polygon—a triangle. The inscribed circle is obtained by bisecting the angles of the triangle. These bisectors pass through a common point which is the center of the inscribed circle.

6. GREAT

Any circle on the surface of a sphere whose plane goes through the center of the sphere is called a great circle. If the earth be considered as a sphere of radius 3,960 miles, the great circles passing through the North and South Poles are called meridians of longitude.

7. OSCULATING

An osculating circle of a curve has three or more coincident points in common with the curve. This term appears to have come into use early in the eighteenth century. The radius of the osculating circle gives the radius of curvature of a curve. This is usually found by making use of a formula in calculus.

8. ESCRIBED

The interior bisector of one angle and the exterior bisectors of the other angles of a triangle are concurrent in a point which is equidistant from one side and the other sides produced of a triangle. Hence, a circle can be described to touch one side and the other sides produced. Such a circle is called an escribed circle of the triangle, and every triangle has three escribed circles.

9. CIRCUMSCRIBED

The meaning of "to circumscribe" is to describe a figure around another so as to touch it at points without cutting it. This is precisely what takes place with the circumscribed circle. To find the center of such a circle, bisect the sides of a triangle and erect perpendiculars. They are concurrent at the circumcenter. The radius R of the circumscribed circle of the triangle ABC is given by

$$R = \frac{a}{2 \sin A} = \frac{b}{2 \sin B} = \frac{c}{2 \sin C}$$

[173]

INDEX